veg

the greengrocer's cookbook

veg

the greengrocer's cookbook

gregg wallace

PHOTOGRAPHS BY SIMON BROWN

MITCHELL BEAZLEY

To Tom and Libby Wallace, my kitchen porters

Veg, The Greengrocer's Cookbook by Gregg Wallace

First published in Great Britain in 2006 by Mitchell Beazley, an imprint of Octopus Publishing Group Limited, 2–4 Heron Quays, London E14 4JP.

© Octopus Publishing Group Limited 2006
Text © Gregg Wallace 2006

A CIP catalogue record for this book is available from the British Library.

ISBN 13: 978 1 845332 24 2
ISBN 10: 1 84533 224 5

While all reasonable care has been taken during the preparation of this edition, neither the publisher, editors, nor the author can accept responsibility for any consequences arising from the use thereof or from the information contained therein.

Commissioning Editor: Rebecca Spry
Executive Art Editors: Yasia Williams and Nicky Collings
Design concept: Miranda Harvey
Design: Lizzie Ballantyne
Editor: Vanessa Kendell
Photography: Simon Brown
Home economy: Zed
Production: Angela Young
Index: John Noble

Typeset in Simoncini Garamond and Scala

It is inadvisable for young children or the elderly to eat uncooked or undercooked eggs.

contents

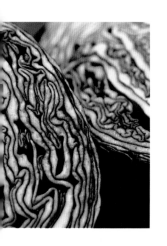

introduction

I have included in this book the veg that are important to me. I am a British greengrocer, so I didn't want to give you a culinary world tour; I just wanted to look at vegetables that will grow here in Britain. Not all the veg are native to these islands, but they all grow here well enough. Every vegetable in this book I have grown or had grown for me, and then sold on to London restaurants.

I firmly believe in buying local produce in season. OK, I enjoy the taste of a banana as much as the next man. In an age of cheap travel, no-one is going to be a culinary purist. I have now reached this conclusion: it's OK to eat an imported vegetable at any time of the year as long as it has no chance of growing in this country. But if it has a season over here, then you should only eat it in that season. You see, all veg is at its best when there's a lot of it. If everybody ate seasonally, we would all eat tastier and cheaper food. That's why I've included seasonal charts in each chapter, showing in green the months during which the chapter's veg is in season.

I am aware that most of us are limited in our shopping options. I haven't listed endless varieties and hybrids, I've only included varieties that most of us are likely to get our hands on. I am a realist. If supermarkets on the whole weren't convenient and at least sometimes good value for money, then no-one would shop in them. But I urge you to try other options for your fresh produce. Farmers markets are spreading, and there are many good farm shops. But if you really want to get your hands on fresh and tasty veg, then grow it yourself. If you can't do that, and I quite understand the concept of limited time, then find out where your local allotment is, arm yourself with a flask of tea and a small bottle of brandy, wander over there and make friends with the growers. Their crop all comes up at once. Every allotment grower I know is desperate for a home for his vegetables. These are the freshest, best veg in town, and every grower can tell you exactly what he's put on his crop. I filmed on allotments from Newcastle to Bristol over the course of a year and I was amazed at the wide social mix of these growers. I am also convinced that the combination of fresh air, light exercise and fresh fruit and vegetables is the recipe for a long and active life.

The recipes in this book are not restaurant recipes. I haven't chosen them because they look pretty; I've chosen them because they are my favourite things to eat and because mostly they're very simple, as a lot of good food is. This is not a book solely for vegetarians, although there are lots of vegetarian recipes in here. I obviously love all veg, but consider myself an enthusiastic carnivore. *The Greengrocer's Cookbook* reflects exactly that. I wanted to pass on years of knowledge and experience and to demonstrate how diverse and fascinating British culinary heritage can be.

I spent the best part of a year cooking the recipes for this book and it was a hugely enjoyable experience. It confirmed to me just how much in love with food, and vegetables in particular, I am. If I could find a way of paying the bills and spending 4 days a week in the kitchen, I would.

These recipes were tried out on anybody who happened to pass my way. My mate Zed tasted most of them, and many were split between my children, Tom and Libby, and my girlfriend, Amanda. I couldn't, even with the help of these people close to me, eat all of the food I was preparing, so I encouraged the locals of nearby pub The Railway Tavern to come and try some!

I have been working with vegetables for a long time now. I've seen many fads and trends come and go. It's really nice to see that we are now looking at our own dishes with the enthusiasm that we previously reserved for foreign cuisines. Our unwillingness to highlight our own food whilst elevating that of other countries has been a mystery to me for many years. When we visit other countries, one of the most enjoyable aspects of the trip is sampling the local cuisine made with good, local, seasonal produce. We know in our hearts that this is the right way to eat. So why is it we admire people in foreign climes who eat the produce they grow, but we refuse to do it when we get home?

I've enjoyed writing this book, waiting for the veg to grow on the farm so I could bring it home and cook it. I don't expect you to copy my example and don your wellies, but I can give you a seasonal guide to the best of British produce, tips on how to buy it, different ways of cooking it, and many recipes for very good home-cooked food. Go on, dig in.

organics

When it comes to veg, what I am concerned about is flavour. I'm not bothered whether my veg is organic or not. I get upset when people claim organic vegetables taste better than non-organic, although I can understand if they're concerned about pesticides (I'm not). For example, I have heard many claims that an organic carrot tastes better than a non-organic carrot. But how can anyone be sure? For a start, what carrot are they talking about? There are more than 500 varieties. Where was it grown? What soil did it sit in? What was it fed? What weather conditions did it experience? And, more importantly, how long has it been out of the ground? All these factors will come into play, but none is more important than the time it has been out of the ground. No-one can convince me that an organic carrot flown in from Azerbaijan is going to taste better than a non-organic one from my Uncle Ted's allotment picked 15 minutes ago. About 4 years ago I visited a supermarket, introduced myself to shoppers and took their organic veg away from them. I asked them where they thought the produce came from. Most believed it to be British. I suspect that they all had a vision of a nice old man working his small-holding. Every packet I looked at was imported.

The word 'pesticides' is an emotive one. A 'pesticide' is just something that kills pests. Some hardy cabbages attract slugs and these slugs can be killed with salty water, so that makes the sea a pesticide. You see my point don't you? Also, the idea that farmers spray expensive solutions over their crops willy nilly isn't true in my experience. But if I've spent the best part of a year nurturing a new type of salad leaf and insects try and get hold of it, it's them or me, and daddy longlegs is going to cop it.

People are rightly wary of GM foods. When the newspapers started reporting on genetic modification, many people ran as far as they could in the opposite direction, straight to organics. Big businesses can't even get them trialled over here. Quite right. We don't know enough about it yet.

I want tasty, local vegetables. Veg starts to die and so lose its flavour as soon as it is picked. There is only one really significant factor when it comes to flavour, and that is the length of time it takes a vegetable to get from the ground to your mouth.

artichokes and cardoons

Globe artichokes are actually thistles. If they are left on the plant they open up and produce beautiful but bristly flowers; the artichoke is the flower bud that hasn't opened yet. For most people the globe artichoke appears to be the scariest of vegetables. It looks impenetrable, and what exactly are you supposed to do with it? I didn't go near one for years. I'd handled them as a youngster in Covent Garden, but it was a long time before I was brave enough to cook one.

globe artichokes

There is heated debate about whether you should eat the whole artichoke or just the heart. I'm in the 'cook it whole' camp; there's delicious flesh in those pointy leaves. I know that the heart is a beautiful thing, but unless people see a whole cooked artichoke and rip off the leaves to get to it they'll never fully understand where it comes from. I love to prise the flesh from each leaf with my front teeth. Many dip their leaves in a vinaigrette, but I just want soft, melted, salty butter on mine.

There are two things to bear in mind with globe artichokes: don't lick your fingers when you're preparing one and wash your hands after you've handled one. Otherwise your fingers will discolour. The other side-effect is that artichokes strip your palate and severely (and not pleasantly) alter the taste of wine. My advice is to drink water with them, and lots of it. And don't touch wine until you're into your main course.

We do grow artichokes in this country, but not on a big scale. They just won't stand frost. The most successful growing areas are around the coastlines, especially the Atlantic.

types of globe artichokes

Globe artichokes come in a range of shapes: some are as round as goldfish bowls, others as long and straight as tulips. They can be green, brown, purple or a mixture of all three. Which you choose is not important. **Baby artichokes** are lovely. They haven't formed the hairy choke on the heart of the bulb that has to be removed, so they can be cooked and eaten whole. They're particularly good with a squeeze of lemon and a hard mature cheese. I've had them flattened, battered and deep-fried.

globe artichokes

jan	feb	mar	apr	may	jun	jul	aug	sep	oct	nov	dec

Jerusalem artichokes

jan	feb	mar	apr	may	jun	jul	aug	sep	oct	nov	dec

cardoons

jan	feb	mar	apr	may	jun	jul	aug	sep	oct	nov	dec

a few facts about globe artichokes

Although cultivated from the wild cardoon, globe artichokes have acquired some very high-brow patronage. Henrietta Maria, Queen of Charles I, was a huge fan. She had a large garden in Wimbledon ripped up and devoted entirely to the globe artichoke.

There is disagreement as to the origin of the globe artichoke; some say it is North Africa, some say Sicily. It must have been farmed from a wild plant in the ancient world. I suppose then you could safely claim that it came from Carthage, seeing as the Carthaginians ruled over both areas. Many claimed the globe artichoke was an aphrodisiac. That's not an unusual claim for a vegetable. What is unusual is that its sexy powers were thought to be so strong that women were forbidden to eat it.

buying and storing globe artichokes

The inner leaves of the artichoke must be tightly bound. Remember, this is a flower bud that will open with age. Even on the freshest 'choke the outer leaves will be separating, but the next layer should be tightly closed. Look at the tips of the outer and top leaves; any discolouring is a sign of age. Globe artichokes won't hold up for very long. Ideally, you want to eat them on the day you buy them. If you do want to store them for 2 or 3 days, put the stem in some water as you would with a flower, then place it in the fridge.

Jerusalem artichokes

I love the earthy flavour of a Jerusalem artichoke. A bowl of steaming ivory-coloured Jerry 'choke soup with a drizzle of truffle oil on top is a great thing. Jerry 'chokes can be earthy and sweet at the same time – clever little fellows. I think they're good-looking and a nice little handful; the vegetable equivalent of a golden nugget.

The Jerusalem artichoke plant can grow to well over 1.5 metres (5-feet) high. It didn't originate anywhere near Jerusalem and it's nothing like (and no relative of) a globe artichoke. A globe artichoke is a type of thistle, while the Jerusalem is a root or tuber. The Jerusalem is related to the sunflower, which must be where it gets its height from.

Jerusalem artichokes do have a drawback though, which is that they cause wind. This is because they contain an indigestible carbohydrate called inulin.

types of Jerusalem artichokes

I used to get the right needle when I was growing fantastic Jerusalem artichokes and finding them difficult to sell. It wasn't that this veg was unpopular; it was on menus all over the place. It's just that mine were elongated, irregularly shaped and knobbly, which made them hard to peel. So instead of buying my home-grown 'chokes, chefs were buying the inferior-tasting, but smoother and more barrel-shaped (and peeler friendly) French ones. I've now managed to source the seeds of a smoother, less knobbly type of 'choke, but I still don't want to grow barrel-shaped dark brown ones.

There is no reason to avoid knobbly 'chokes. If they are hard to peel, boil them for 8 minutes, then peel. As soon as you remove the skins the veg starts to turn murky grey, so have a bowl of acidulated water to hand to drop them into.

a few facts about Jerusalem artichokes

The French call the Jerusalem artichoke *topinambour*. The 'choke hit the Parisian markets in the 17th century, at the same time as a small group of South American Indians were being presented at court. These Indians, from the Topinambour tribe, were a hit and Parisian greengrocers linked their new root veg to the Indians by naming it after them. The fact that this tribe lived somewhere near Brazil, and the Jerry 'choke came from Canada and North America, didn't seem to bother them.

The first Europeans to lay eyes on Jerusalem artichokes were French explorers, who saw Red Indians growing them in Massachusetts. Explorer Samuel de Champlain said they tasted of artichokes, which explains the 'artichoke' part of the name. As for the 'Jerusalem' bit, the 'choke is related to a sunflower, and the Italian for sunflower is '*girasole*', from which comes 'Jerusalem'. Another theory is that the name comes from the Dutch town Terneuzen, from where the first Jerry 'chokes landed in England came.

cardoons

Cardoons should be erect with no browning around the edges. They are big, and therefore hard to store. Chop them up and keep them in the fridge for up to a week.

buying and storing Jerusalem artichokes

The artichoke must be firm and hard; any give or sponginess is a bad thing. Kept in the cool and dark, Jerusalem artichokes should hold up for at least a week.

preparing and boiling globe artichokes

Cut the stalk off close to the base and slice off the top quarter. Peel away the outer leaves and trim the top third of all the leaves with scissors. Drop each artichoke into acidulated water as you go. Bring a large pan of salted water to the boil. Add the veg and a squeeze of lemon and boil for 30–45 minutes, until the base is tender to a knife point and a leaf pulls away easily from the bottom. Drain upside down and shake. Spread the leaves and remove the small inner ones and the hairy choke underneath. Try with: vinaigrette, melted butter or hollandaise sauce.

frying and simmering baby globe artichokes

Wash the artichokes, trim the stalks and peel. Cut into quarters lengthways and drop into acidulated water. Heat 2 tbsp olive oil in a frying pan. Add the veg and cook over a medium heat until browned. Add a crushed garlic clove if you like. When brown, pour in 150–200ml (5-7fl oz) veg stock, cover and simmer until cooked, 10–15 minutes. Try with: squeezed lemon juice and pecorino cheese.

preparing and boiling Jerusalem artichokes

Scrub the artichokes with a brush, then peel them thinly. Drop them into acidulated water as you go. (If they are very knobbly, peel when cooked.) Bring a large pan of salted water to the boil. Add the artichokes and a squeeze of lemon and boil, lid off, for 12–15 minutes, until cooked. Drain, run under a cold tap and peel away the skins. Try: fried in butter for 10 minutes.

puréeing Jerusalem artichokes

Follow the instructions for preparing and boiling. Rub the veg through a sieve into a pan with a knob of butter. Add a little single cream and a grating of nutmeg and stir. Try with: a pork chop.

roasting Jerusalem artichokes

Preheat the oven to 190°C/375°F/gas mark 5. Scrub the artichokes, but do not peel. Bring a pan of salted water to the boil and par-boil the veg for 5 minutes. Drain and add to a preheated roasting tin with 2 tbsp of vegetable oil. Roast for 30 minutes. Try with: a roasted joint.

preparing and boiling cardoons

Bring a pan of salted water to the boil. Clean the cardoon's base. Cut off the hard stems and remove the tender stalks. Cut these into 6cm (2½ inch) chunks. Sprinkle over lemon juice. Cut the hearts into quarters. Boil stems and hearts for 6–12 minutes. Try with: butter.

globe artichoke with tomato vinaigrette

Before I tasted this vinaigrette I always ate my artichokes with melted butter. This is much more civilized, tastier and better for you – it's how an artichoke should be cooked and served. But make sure you use all the artichoke; throwing away those plump-fleshed leaves and concentrating on the heart is a crime.

serves 4

4 globe artichokes

salt

juice of 2 lemons

2 tbsp red wine vinegar

12 tbsp olive oil

2 tsp caster sugar

2 tsp chopped dill

3 large ripe tomatoes, peeled and chopped (keep the seeds)

Prepare the artichokes by cutting off the stalks, slicing off the top quarters, removing the outer leaves and trimming the rest.

Bring a large pan of salted water to the boil, then add the artichokes and a tablespoon of lemon juice.

Boil for 30–45 minutes, until the bases are tender and the larger leaves come away easily. Meanwhile, combine the remaining lemon juice with the vinegar, olive oil, sugar, dill and tomatoes.

Drain the artichokes and shake well. Allow the artichokes to cool, then spread the leaves and remove the small inner leaves together with the hairy choke.

Pour the dressing over the artichoke to serve.

stoved Jerusalem artichokes

This is an old, old recipe which gives us a chance to feature this nutty vegetable as the star of the dish rather than relegate it to a bit part.

serves 6

25g (1oz) butter

2 tbsp olive oil

1kg (2lb 4oz) Jerusalem artichokes, scrubbed and halved

1 tbsp finely chopped parsley

salt and black pepper

Heat the butter and oil over a medium heat in a large non-stick pan. When the butter stops foaming, add the artichokes. Put the lid on, but leave it slightly open. Cook for about 5 minutes, then turn them carefully. This is to part-fry and part-steam them.

Cook for a further 5 minutes, then remove the lid and check if the artichokes are cooked through; they should be soft and browned. Sprinkle over the parsley and season before serving.

asparagus

Without doubt, asparagus is one of the luxury
vegetables. Expensive most certainly, but there's
nothing quite like popping buttered asparagus
into your mouth, savouring the soft slippery surface
and biting down on the firm interior of these
uniquely flavoured spears. Eating a plate of
asparagus makes you realise there is a benevolent
supreme being who is concerned about our welfare.
Asparagus is expensive to buy because it's expensive
to cultivate. An asparagus plant, newly planted,
will take three years to produce spears that are
good enough to sell.

Then it will only produce these spears for another 3 years. So, a typical asparagus field will only give a yield 50 per cent of the time. Also, a field will only produce about 1 spear for each square foot, which means growers employ a lot of land for such a small vegetable. Furthermore, the harvesting of this delicacy is back-breaking; each spear must be hand-cut, as there is no way to mechanically harvest it. What would be your daily rate for working, bent double, in an asparagus field?

I love veg served in the simplest way possible, and asparagus is the pinnacle of this love. Cooked, it virtually resembles raw. Veg meets pan, pan meets veg. That's it, not veg meets pan and goes on a trip for the weekend.

types of asparagus

Asparagus is usually graded well. It starts with pencil-thin '**sprue**', leading to thumb-sized '**jumbo**', with '**extra select**', '**select**' and '**medium**' the 3 grades in between.

White asparagus is a peculiar thing. I think so, but then I'm in a minority. I'm used to the green stuff, and I find white asparagus low in both texture and flavour. It is only Britain, Italy and parts of the USA that eat their asparagus green. The rest of the world, and that includes most of Europe, eats it white. An asparagus spear that rises above the soil turns green. To keep it white, you have to build up the earth around it as it grows, keeping it underground and out of the light. You prepare the white as you do the green.

a few facts about asparagus

Asparagus was most certainly eaten by the ancient Greeks, who must have gathered it as a wild plant. It was the Romans who first grew asparagus on a large scale, exporting their knowledge of it to the far reaches of their empire. The Romans loved asparagus, with Cato remarking that it was the 'only vegetable worth growing besides cabbage'.

With the decline of the Roman Empire, mass cultivation stopped. Asparagus farming, if it survived at all, would have been on a very small localised scale, but asparagus would have survived as a wild plant. It was the European cult of monasticism, and the monasteries drive for self-sufficiency, that lead to efficient farming once more.

It was during the Renaissance that asparagus became that must-have luxury

| jan | feb | mar | apr | may | jun | jul | aug | sep | oct | nov | dec |

vegetable. 16th century landowners, in what is now the Veneto, made so much money that asparagus became the major crop, replacing corn and flax.

In England, asparagus-growing was given a huge boost with the arrival of the Huguenots. Many of these French Protestant farmers decided a life of asparagus-growing in culturally backward Britain was preferable to persecution and a grizzly death in enlightened France.

Samuel Pepys records in his diary shopping for 'sparrow grass'. The term 'grass' is still used today by growers and traders of asparagus.

buying asparagus

The British asparagus season normally lasts from May to July. With a particularly warm spring, asparagus could be available in late April and remnants may be found in mid-August, but this is unlikely. You will, however, get decent Spanish asparagus before and after the season, but it's not as good as home-grown.

Size matters: for the best bargains aim for jumbo asparagus. These are the fattest stems. Asparagus is sold on weight and jumbo weighs the most per spear. Chefs who want to put a healthy display of spears on a plate but only want to give 200g (7oz) per portion go for thinner spears – serving jumbo might mean only 3 stems on a plate.

Firm spears are what we want. When you hold the base of the spear between your thumb and forefinger, the asparagus should stand to attention. Any wobbling around is a sign of ageing. The skin of the spear should be smooth; asparagus wrinkles with age, giving long thin wrinkles that get deeper and longer as the spear continues to deteriorate.

Have a good look at the heads too; they should be closed tight. A head that is opening up is not the freshest. The top of the head should not feel wet, but neither should it be bone dry.

Don't concern yourself with the colour of asparagus so long as it's green (not white). Dark green is no guarantee of freshness, and neither are purple heads. Very pale grass with light tips will taste as good as those that are emerald green with purple tips.

You should observe how much of your expensive spears you will have to discard. The tough bit or woodiness always starts at the base, but how far up is our tree growing? We have waited all year for our 8 weeks of asparagus and we want it perfect! Hold the midpoint of a spear in your fingers and wiggle it; the top should wiggle. Move your fingers down the spear and repeat the process. When you get to a bit that doesn't wiggle, you need to chop it off.

storing asparagus

Asparagus is best eaten within minutes, or at worst hours, of picking. It starts to deteriorate the minute it is picked. Very fresh asparagus will keep refrigerated for up to 5 days, but be warned that it loses its flavour by the hour.

raw asparagus

Eating freshly cut asparagus raw is not unknown, but it's not something I'd recommend. Just cut away or break off the woody bits from the bottom of the stems.

boiling asparagus

This is by far the best way to cook your asparagus. Cut away or break off the woody bits from the bottom of the stems. Bring a large pan of salted water to the boil and once you have a good rolling boil, add the asparagus. Boil, lid off, for 3–5 minutes, depending on the age and thickness of the spears. Remove from the pan and drain in a colander.

Try with: melted butter or a soft-boiled or poached egg and nothing else. Asparagus is not an accompaniment; it is the star of the show.

griddling asparagus

Discard the woody bits from the bottom of the stems. Bring a large pan of salted water to the boil and once you have a good rolling boil, add the asparagus. Boil, lid off, for 2–4 minutes, depending on the age and thickness of the spears. Remove from the pan and drain in a colander. Heat a griddle pan over a high heat. Brush the asparagus spears with olive oil and when the pan is hot, put them on the griddle and cook for 1–2 minutes, turning regularly.

Try with: hollandaise sauce or Parmesan shavings and balsamic vinegar.

steaming asparagus

If you have a steamer, by all means use it. But you can't discern between lightly boiled and steamed asparagus, so I wouldn't fiddle with it. Cut away the woody bits from the bottom of the stems and put the asparagus in a sieve. Bring a pan of salted water to the boil and wait for plenty of steam to build up before adding the asparagus. Sit the sieve over the pan of boiling water (ensure it doesn't touch the water) and cover with a lid. Cook for 8–15 minutes, depending on the age and thickness of the spears.

Try with: melted butter.

asparagus mousse

This is a very sophisticated dish. It should be prepared at the end of the asparagus season, when all you can get are bent and misshapen spears that look terribly sad, with their heads drying and opening.

serves 4
about 800g (1lb 12oz) asparagus
4 sheets of leaf gelatine
1 egg white
175ml (6fl oz) double cream
salt and white pepper

Snap the woody ends off the asparagus and discard. Chop the remaining stems into 3cm (1¼ inch) pieces.

Bring a pan of salted water to the boil. Drop in the asparagus and cook for about 6–8 minutes until very tender (softer than how you would eat it). You should have 600g (1lb 5oz) of asparagus once you've done this.

Meanwhile, soak the gelatine in a little cold water for about 10 minutes or until completely floppy.

Drain the asparagus, reserve half the cooking water, and liquidize the tender stems. Pour the purée into a measuring jug and add enough of the cooking water to make 600ml (1 pint).

Add the squeezed-out gelatine sheets to the purée and stir well until dissolved. Cool, then chill until the mixture starts to set around the edges.

Beat the egg white until stiff, and softly beat the cream. Season the mousse with salt and pepper, then fold in the egg white until all the egg is incorporated. Fold in the cream, then pour into a serving dish and chill.

asparagus with poached duck egg

A truly elegant starter, this dish heralds spring and is evocative of early summers and lazy suppers on a terrace. Dipping spears of grass into runny egg yolk, drinking rich and fruity white Burgundy....

serves 4
1 tbsp white wine vinegar
4 duck eggs
28 spears of medium asparagus
black pepper

Bring 2 pans of salted water to the boil and pour the vinegar into 1 of them.

Crack the eggs into individual ramekins but don't allow the yolks to break.

Boil the asparagus in the plain water for 3–5 minutes. Turn the other pan down to a bare simmer and gently drop the eggs into the water. Let them cook for 4 minutes.

Drain the asparagus and divide between 4 serving plates. Lift the eggs out with a slotted spoon and lay on top of the asparagus.

Serve with a good grinding of black pepper.

aubergine

The aubergine is celebrated in warmer climes from the Mediterranean to India right through to Australia. Perhaps the most celebrated aubergine dish, eaten all over the Arab world, is imam bayildi. In Europe, the Greeks make moussaka and the French ratatouille, and you can't sit down in southern Italy without being given a plate of *melanzane parmigiana* (a dish of aubergine and Parmesan). It's not surprising that this vegetable is more popular in places that get plenty of sunshine. Aubergines will grow in Britain – indeed I have had them grow very successfully – but only under glass.

One of the most frequently asked questions that arises whenever aubergines are discussed on *Veg Talk* is 'do aubergines need salting?'. The answer is no, they don't. In days gone by, we often cooked with very bitter varieties, and salting would relieve this bitterness. Modern aubergine varieties have had the bitterness bred out of them. Old aubergines can become bitter, but then my advice would be to avoid buying old or wrinkled aubergines. If you are forced to use an old one, then do salt it.

There is one exception to this rule: salting is a good idea if you are going to fry the aubergines as they are legendary for the amount of oil they swallow up, and salting helps prevent this.

Botanically speaking, the aubergine is classified as a fruit, so it shouldn't really be in this book at all. But how can you write a veg book without mentioning aubergines?

types of aubergine

There are many varieties of aubergine, and it would be a tortuous and largely unhelpful job to list them all. **Cyprus aubergine** is the term used by traders in Covent Garden Market (where I used to have a stall) for smaller and more elongated aubergines, which are shaped rather like bananas. They have a slightly sweeter taste than their bigger, rounder brothers. **Violetti** are big and round and are the only aubergines I want. They have very dense flesh, a fairly strong flavour and no seeds. They are sold to restaurants for at least twice the price of a standard aubergine, and are the darlings of the aubergine family.

Pea aubergines are tiny little green babies, the size of a fat pea, and much loved by exponents of Thai cookery. They are extremely bitter and rock hard, and take a fair amount of cooking. Also popular in South-East Asian cookery are **White aubergines**, which are sometimes referred to as 'ping-pong' for obvious reasons. They are not as bitter as the 'pea', but nowhere near as mild as the European aubergine.

a few facts about aubergines

The aubergine, in its wild form, originates from India although the earliest records of cultivation come from China and go back to the 5th century BC. It was not known in Europe until the 13th century, and even then it was not cultivated until the 16th century. It entered the Middle East from Asia and was brought to southern Europe by

| jan | feb | mar | apr | may | jun | jul | aug | sep | oct | nov | dec |

the Arabs. But even in the warmer climes of southern Europe, it was a long while before it became popular, possibly because it is related to the deadly nightshade.

The Americans call aubergines 'eggplant', but in fact it was the English who gave them that name. The first aubergines to hit our shores were white and egg-shaped, hence the name. John Parkinson, an Englishman writing in the 17th century, recommended his countrymen boil aubergines first in vinegar. And we wonder why the rest of Europe laughs at our food! He went on to claim aubergines were a cure for leprosy, piles and stinking breath. The mind boggles.

buying aubergines

Hold the aubergine in your palm; it should feel very heavy for its size. Also check the skin and make sure it hasn't puckered or wrinkled.

storing aubergines

Aubergines will keep in the fridge for up to a week.

griddling aubergines

Cut the green stalks from the aubergines, then slice them into rough 1cm (½ inch) rounds. Drizzle olive oil over both sides of each round. Heat a griddle pan over a medium heat and when the pan is hot, add the aubergine slices – be careful not to overload the pan. Turn regularly until a fork passes through them without resistance.
Try with: aïoli or lamb chops.

roasting aubergines

Preheat the oven to 200°C/400°F/gas mark 6. Cut the green stalks from the aubergines and then halve them lengthways. Score the halves across diagonally, to create a crisscross, but don't cut the skin. Put the aubergines in a roasting dish cut side up and drizzle over a good amount of olive oil – enough to cover the surface. Roast for about 30 minutes until a fork passes through without resistance.
Try with: a tomato and garlic sauce or minced meat.

Imam bayildi

Imam bayildi translates as 'the priest fainted'. Apparently, the imam tasted it and swooned. Who can blame him? The first time I tasted this dish was at Chez Bruce in Wandsworth Common, London. I've tasted many imam bayildis since, and this is the only one that has recreated that delightful first experience.

serves 4

5 tbsp sunflower oil

1 large onion, finely chopped

3 cloves of garlic, crushed

2 tbsp turmeric

2 tbsp ground cumin

2 tbsp ground coriander

2 tbsp mild curry powder

3 aubergines

400g tin chopped tomatoes

50g (1³/₄oz) sultanas

150g (5¹/₂oz) Greek yoghurt, to serve

bunch of mint, to serve

Heat a heavy-based pan over a low heat and add the sunflower oil. When the oil is hot, add the onion and garlic and fry until soft.

Sprinkle over the spices and cook for another 2 minutes, stirring all the time.

Cut the aubergines into cubes the size of a dice, then add these and the tomatoes to the onion mixture. Cover and simmer for 45 minutes, stirring occasionally.

Add the sultanas and cook, lid on, for another 10 minutes.

Remove from the heat and allow to cool. Refrigerate for 24 hours.

Serve cold with Greek yoghurt and mint.

aubergine fritters with tzatziki

It is important to salt here, as aubergines are notorious for soaking up an ocean of oil – salting and rinsing them beforehand prevents this from happening.

serves 4

3 aubergines, sliced into rounds

salt and black pepper

1 egg

115g (4oz) plain flour

¹/₂ tsp cayenne pepper

vegetable oil, for deep-frying

200g (7oz) Greek yoghurt

3cm (1¹/₄ inch) piece of cucumber, finely diced

2 spring onions, thinly sliced

3 tbsp chopped mint

1 clove of garlic, crushed

Put the aubergine rounds in a colander, sprinkle with salt and leave to sit for about 20 minutes.

In a large bowl, whisk 120ml (4fl oz) of water with the egg. Add the flour, cayenne and seasoning to taste, and whisk until smooth.

Rinse the aubergines and pat them dry with kitchen towel. Heat the oil in a large heavy-based pan until a cube of bread dropped in browns in 1 minute. Dip the aubergine rounds into the batter, then deep-fry until brown and crisp. Drain on kitchen towel.

To make the tzatziki, whisk the yoghurt in a bowl until smooth. Add the cucumber, spring onions, mint and garlic. Season well and mix to combine. Serve with the fritters.

moussaka

This is my version of moussaka – it's not hard to make, and it tastes great.

serves 4

450g (1lb) aubergines
salt and black pepper
50ml (2fl oz) olive oil
1 onion, finely chopped
3 cloves of garlic, finely chopped
675g (1lb 8oz) minced lamb
1 tbsp plain flour
400g tin chopped tomatoes
1 tbsp tomato purée
1 tsp caster sugar
2 tbsp chopped oregano
2 tbsp chopped parsley
450g (1lb) tomatoes, sliced
300g (10^1/$_2$oz) natural yoghurt
2 eggs
50g (1^3/$_4$oz) Parmesan, grated
25g (1oz) Cheddar, grated

Slice the aubergines into rounds and place in a colander. Sprinkle with salt and leave to sit for about 20 minutes, before rinsing and drying them on kitchen towel. This process reduces the amount of oil absorbed by the aubergines.

Heat the oil in a large pan or frying pan over a medium heat. Add the onion and garlic and fry until soft. Add the lamb, turn up the heat, and cook until brown. Stir in the flour, tinned tomatoes, tomato purée, sugar and herbs and season to taste. Bring to the boil and simmer, lid off, for 20 minutes.

Preheat the oven to 180°C/350°F/gas mark 4.

Arrange half the aubergine slices in a large, shallow dish, then layer half the tomato slices on top followed by half the meat mixture. Repeat the layers until all the ingredients are used up.

Beat together the yoghurt, eggs and cheeses. Season and pour over the meat. Bake for 40 minutes, until golden and bubbling.

baby aubergine salad

Pine nuts, currants, chilli and aubergine are a very good combination. I make a big bowlful of this, leave it in the fridge, and happily munch on it every time I get a beer out.

serves 4

12 baby aubergines, halved lengthways
125ml (4fl oz) olive oil
juice of 1 lemon
2 tbsp sherry vinegar
25g (1oz) pine nuts
25g (1oz) currants
1 tbsp caster sugar
^{1}/$_2$ red chilli, finely chopped
2 bay leaves
salt and black pepper

Preheat the grill to its highest setting. Brush the halved aubergines with a little olive oil and grill, cut-side down, for about 5 minutes. Turn them over and grill for another 5 minutes, until blackened in spots.

Mix together the remaining oil, the lemon juice, vinegar, pine nuts, currants, sugar, chilli, bay leaves, and salt and pepper to taste.

Put the hot aubergines in a serving bowl and pour over the dressing. Leave to cool, turning a couple of times. Serve cold.

beans

Beans are some of the most important and widely used vegetables in the world. We have eaten them for ever, first picking them wild, then harvesting them. The historical importance of beans, fresh and dried, as part of our diet cannot be overstated. The term 'full of beans' bears witness to this. Beans are technically legumes, but then so are peas and lentils. So, what we are dealing with here is a legume that isn't a pea or a lentil. There are two categories of beans: fleshy pods and seeds. Fleshy pods are those edible pods such as French beans, and seeds refers to extracted beans such as broad beans.

I have nothing against dried, or in some cases, tinned beans, but as I'm a trader in fresh produce, I am only covering fresh beans here. They are among the world's most widely cultivated vegetables, which is amazing as they are a New World crop and came to Europe in what Felipe Fernandez-Armesto refers to as the Colombian exchange. In fact, all beans apart from broad beans share one key historical fact: they were domesticated over 5,000 years ago in what is now Central and South America.

borlotti beans

One of the most beautiful beans, the borlotti has a truly lovely red and white marbling effect on the pod. Even the beans, which have the same marbling effect in black, look like they are trying to stay as beautiful as they can for as long as they can. In fact, it's a shame they taste so good because when they are cooked you lose all that beauty. I like the look of them so much that, when in season, I keep them in the kitchen in jars to gaze at.

Borlotti beans are mostly sold dried, but I urge you to get your hands on the fresh ones, if you can. They are Italy's most popular beans, and in France (where they are given the delightful name of *rose-cocos*) they are loved, too.

borlotti beans

| jan | feb | mar | apr | may | jun | jul | aug | sep | oct | nov | dec |

broad beans

| jan | feb | mar | apr | may | jun | jul | aug | sep | oct | nov | dec |

cannellini beans

| jan | feb | mar | apr | may | jun | jul | aug | sep | oct | nov | dec |

French beans

| jan | feb | mar | apr | may | jun | jul | aug | sep | oct | nov | dec |

runner beans

| jan | feb | mar | apr | may | jun | jul | aug | sep | oct | nov | dec |

When buying borlotti beans, look for bright red, vibrant colours. The whole bean will discolour as a result of ageing, the colour fading day by day after it has been picked.

cooking borlotti beans

Bring a pan of unsalted water to the boil (there should be enough to cover the beans by at least 7.5cm/3 inches). Drop in the fresh beans and boil, lid off, for 45-50 minutes. Taste to see if they are soft.

Try with: pork.

broad beans

The broad bean (or fava bean) is probably my favourite bean. It is incredibly versatile and there is something about its mealy texture that seriously appeals to me. The size of the broad bean alone is impressive – all that flesh in a vegetable. When I'm cooking them (which I often do), I have to prepare many more than I need, as I steal so many before serving.

China is now the world's leading producer of them. In Italy, the immature beans are eaten with pecorino cheese. In the States, they are mixed with corn to make the dish called succotash. Farmers like growing broad beans because they feed nitrogen back into the soil – clever old beans! They are hardy little chaps, too. Sown in autumn, they survive the winter frosts and are ready to harvest in early summer. Savory is a common flavouring for broad beans, which growers plant alongside the bean to attract the black fly thus keeping it away from their moneyed crop.

We grow lots of broad beans at the farm. They compete with runner beans as one of the prettiest of all growing plants. But the major problem I have every year is getting the pickers to pick the pods at the right size. I only want the small and tender ones for my dinner plate, and so do all the chefs that I supply. The pickers, however, desperate to make 100kg (220lb), will pick all the old, big, fat ones and leave the young, tender ones until they get bigger.

Shelling broad beans has a downside, which is that your fingers can go black. And, if you accidentally put your finger in your mouth while shelling the beans, the disgusting taste will guarantee that you will be doubly careful next time.

A lot of cooks claim that the big broad beans need skinning after cooking and the small ones don't. You don't want to mess up your bowl of beans because you're undecided whether they are big or small, so my advice is to skin them all.

types of broad beans

Broad beans come in 2 types: the **Windsor**, with 4 seeds inside a short pod, and the **Longpod**, containing 8 or more. All in all, there are nearly 40 popular cultivated varieties of broad beans, but, from a cook's point of view, there is nothing to distinguish between them.

a few facts about broad beans

Broad beans have the honour of being mentioned by Homer and were actually found in excavations of Troy. They have been food for man and beast since the Bronze Age. It is probable, but not proven, that they came from the Middle East. Certainly they have been a European staple for centuries. Broad beans are the only beans native to the Old World. They were taken to America and probably passed all the other beans travelling in the opposite direction.

The ancient Egyptians regarded broad beans as unclean (funny people the ancient Egyptians, they also worshipped onions). Herodotus claimed that the priests didn't even look at them. I mean, what could happen if you accidentally looked at a bean? The followers of Pythagoras were forbidden to eat broad beans. No one really knows why. It is possible that he thought the souls of the dead had migrated into them.

The beans were eaten by the Romans at funerals and, in fact, the word 'beano' was originally used by the ancient Celts for a funeral 'beanfeast'. They were one of the most important crops throughout the medieval period, particularly because they could be so successfully dried, and the penalty for bean-stealing in the Middle Ages was death.

buying broad beans

When buying, discard any split pods. Colour is not an issue here; some pods are very dark green and some are light green, it's just how it goes. But what you do want is as slender a pod as possible; slender pods mean young, slender beans inside.

storing broad beans

Broad beans will store quite happily in a refrigerator for a week. Of course, this always depends on how fresh they were when you bought them. My advice is to eat them within 4 days of purchasing. A broad bean also freezes extremely well – that little outer skin protects the flesh fantastically.

cooking broad beans

Very young broad beans, of less than 7.5cm (3 inches) long, can be eaten whole in the pods, and only need a wash before being cooked. But usually the beans have to be podded. If the beans are getting on a bit, they will need skinning after cooking too.

To boil broad beans, bring a pan of unsalted water to the boil. Drop in the beans and boil, lid off, for 4 minutes – this will work for whole baby pods and for podded older beans. Try one of the podded beans; if the skins are tough, then cool them under running water and drain before peeling off the skins and reheating the beans in a pan with a little butter. If serving the beans with the skin on, just drain and serve with butter.

To steam broad beans (this method is for whole baby pods and young podded beans), melt a large knob of butter in a pan over a high heat with 2–3 tbsp of vegetable or chicken stock per 300g (10½oz) beans. As soon as this reaches a boil, add the beans and cover. Cook over a medium heat for 6–7 minutes, stirring occasionally to prevent the beans from sticking.

To cream, add 2 tbsp of single cream once the beans are cooked.

Try with: savory.

cannellini beans

The cannellini bean is a very popular bean in Italy, and is a special favourite of the Tuscans. Many more cannellini beans are sold dried than fresh. The cannellini is a white bean and rather like the kidney bean. The beans are held within a long, thin, attractive yellow skin. Unbeknown, I should imagine, to many Italians, is the fact that this bean originated in the area that is now Argentina. Darina Allen, in her *Ballymaloe Cookery Course*, has them completely interchangeable with borlotti beans, and I can see no reason why this should not be so. When buying, look for a bright, canary yellow bean – if it's fading to white it's ageing. Also, feel the ends; these get soft before the middle does and lose their roundness.

cooking cannellini beans

Bring a pan of unsalted water to the boil (there should be enough to cover the beans by at least 7.5cm/3 inches). Drop in the fresh beans and boil, lid off, for 45–50 minutes. Taste to see if they are soft.

Try with: pork.

French beans

The French bean has many identities. I have never known one vegetable to be called so many names: string, snap, haricot vert, green…. French beans are the most popular beans among the restaurants I sell to, and when I had a stall at Covent Garden Market we shifted them by the ton. I don't know how they got the name 'French' because, apart from the ones I've seen growing in England, every French bean I've ever come across has come from Kenya. Kenya is also a big producer of flowers, and, in the build-up to Mother's Day and Valentine's Day, flowers are at such a premium that the cargo planes coming out of Kenya are stuffed full of them, leaving no room for the beans – so they tend to be expensive and unimpressive around these times of year.

types of French beans

French beans come in green or yellow. There are big ones, but the variety you usually see is the **dwarf bean**. The French believe the yellow ones are sweeter but, as with all vegetables, if you want sweet you want young and fresh. I have seen **yellow French beans** sold over here, but they are usually twice the size of the normal dwarf French and are usually grown in France rather than Kenya. A **bobby bean** is actually just a big, fat variety of French bean – not widely available – but I love them. I suspect the reason I enjoy them so much more than the dwarf French bean is because I'm so used to seeing imported French beans that I rather welcome the fresher, crunchier home-grown bobby.

buying French beans

Look for bright colour and firmness. A drooping bean is no use to anybody.

cooking French beans

Trim off the tops, but there is no need to remove the skinny tails.

To boil, bring a pan of salted water to the boil. Drop in the beans and boil, lid off, for 4–5 minutes. They should still retain a slight crunch. Drain and serve with butter.

To steam, melt a large knob of butter in a pan over a high heat with 2–3 tbsp of vegetable or chicken stock per 300g (10½oz) beans. As soon as this reaches a boil, add the beans and cover. Cook over a medium heat for 4–5 minutes, shaking the pan occasionally to prevent the beans from sticking.

Try with: pork chops.

runner beans

Originally named 'scarlet runners' on account of their beautiful flowers, runner beans growing on frames are a vision to behold. It is said that they got the name 'runner' from the speed with which they climb up the frame.

The texture and flavour of the runner bean doesn't quite match the beauty of its flower. Its taste takes some getting used to, but I recommend you persevere. What I first perceived as coarse I now enjoy as crisp, and what was once bland is now juicy.

American Indians ate the roots of wild runner beans rather than the beans themselves. There is evidence of cultivation in Mexico over 2,000 years ago. It is believed that the wild plants were pollinated by humming birds as well as bees. The first evidence we have of them growing in Britain is from the journal of John Tradescant, gardener to Charles I. Unfortunately, he had no interest in the bean and grew them purely for the flowers, so his beans became headless (as did his employer). No one seems to have cooked runner beans at all until the early 18th century, when we have records of them being eaten from Chelsea gardener, Philip Miller.

Buy runner beans as small as possible – the bigger they get the rougher and tougher they get. Rub your forefinger over them, because, while all runner beans have a rough texture, they get a lot rougher with age. It's like the difference between a man's chin in the evening and a man's chin who hasn't shaved for 3 days.

cooking runner beans

Top and tail the beans, then pull the strings off the sides, if necessary. Slice thinly or use a bean slicer.

To boil, drop the sliced beans into boiling, salted water and cook for 8–10 minutes. They should still retain a slight crunch. Drain and serve with butter.

To steam, melt a large knob of butter in a pan over a high heat with 2–3 tbsp of vegetable or chicken stock per 300g (10½oz) beans. As soon as this reaches a boil, add the beans and cover. Cook for 2–3 minutes, shaking the pan occasionally to prevent sticking.

Try with: shepherd's pie.

broad bean and parsley sauce with boiled bacon

This is truly the way I love to eat: stunningly moist pig, soft veg and a creamy sauce. Food like this brings joy to my soul – I look at the plate and see centuries of simple, excellent British culinary tradition. Cry 'God for England, Harry and St. George'!

serves 4

1.5kg (3lb 5oz) unsmoked bacon collar

3 cloves of garlic, left whole

3 bay leaves

3 carrots, roughly chopped

2 onions, roughly chopped

3 celery stalks, roughly chopped

2 tsp thyme leaves

400g (14oz) shelled broad beans (1kg/2lb 4oz in the pod)

50g (1³/₄oz) butter

50g (1³/₄oz) plain flour

300ml (10fl oz) full-fat milk

1¹/₂ tbsp chopped parsley

5 tbsp double cream

Wash the gammon, pat dry with kitchen towel and place in a large, heavy-bottomed pan. Cover with water. Add the garlic, bay leaves, carrots, onions, celery and thyme. Bring to the boil, then reduce the heat, cover and simmer for 1¹/₂ hours, topping up with boiling water if necessary.

Meanwhile, bring a pan of water to the boil, add the broad beans and boil for 2 minutes. Do not salt the water. Drain in a colander and rinse under a cold tap. Peel off the skins.

Melt the butter in another pan and gradually stir in the flour. When smooth, slowly pour in the milk. Cook, stirring all the time. Remove from the heat and add the beans and parsley.

Lift the meat out of the pan and trim off excess fat. Drain the vegetables and discard the herbs you can see. Warm the sauce and add the cream. Serve alongside the bacon and vegetables.

broad beans in yoghurt

I love Greek yoghurt. It complements so many other flavours. You have to be careful with broad beans though, as their subtle flavour is lost in anything too strong. I've made this dish so many times and I'm confident that I finally have the best balance of ingredients!

serves 4

400g (14oz) shelled broad beans (1kg/2lb 4oz in the pod)

1 shallot, finely chopped

2 tsp chopped mint

juice of ¹/₂ lemon

400g (14oz) Greek yoghurt

1 tbsp chopped chives, to serve

Bring a pan of water to the boil, add the broad beans and boil for 2 minutes. Do not salt the water. Drain in a colander and rinse under a cold tap. Peel off the skins.

Combine all the ingredients, except for the chives, in a serving bowl. To serve, scatter over the chopped chives.

broad beans and bacon

This is a plate of sticky goodness. The sweetness of the beans really complements the saltiness of the bacon. I would be more than happy to eat a bucketful of it.

serves 4

1 tbsp olive oil

1 shallot, finely chopped

80g (2¼oz) bacon lardons

400g (14oz) shelled broad beans (1kg/2lb 4oz in the pod)

2 little gem lettuces, chopped

75ml (2½fl oz) chicken or vegetable stock

50ml (2fl oz) crème fraîche

2 tbsp chopped chervil

salt and black pepper

Heat the oil in a large pan over a medium heat. Fry the shallot and lardons until the shallot is soft.

Add the shelled beans and chopped lettuces, then cover and fry gently for 6 minutes.

Stir in the stock, crème fraîche, chervil and seasoning to taste. Cook, uncovered, over a low heat for about 15 minutes. Stir occasionally and gently, so as not to break the beans. Serve straight away.

French beans in tomato sauce with lamb

I adore mint sauce, and have searched long and hard for an alternative way to serve lamb. This hasn't been easy as I love this combination, but here's another of my favourite lamb dishes. The French beans add a fine crunch to the meat.

serves 4

1 tbsp vegetable oil

4 shallots, finely chopped

4 cloves of garlic, crushed

2 x 400g tins chopped tomatoes

salt

300g (10½oz) French beans, topped and quartered

8 lamb chops

1 tbsp olive oil

Heat the vegetable oil in a pan over a medium heat. Add the shallots, then cover and sweat for 3 minutes. Stir in the garlic and cook for another 30 seconds.

Add the tomatoes and simmer, uncovered, until the liquor has reduced by half. Remove from the heat.

Meanwhile, bring a pan of salted water to the boil. Add the beans and boil for 3 minutes. Drain and stir into the tomato mixture.

Heat a griddle pan over a high heat and brush the chops with olive oil. Put the chops in the hot pan and cook for about 10 minutes on each side, depending on thickness, until cooked and charred.

Serve with the French beans in tomato sauce.

borlotti beans with braised pork

I adore the food of southern Italy. I included this dish for its obvious nod to the purity of dishes, and respect given to ingredients by the good people of *Italiasud*. At first glance you may think this could be a dry dish, but believe me it's not. I first encountered the cooking of pig in milk with chef Alastair Little – a chap who knows a thing or two about *la cucina Italia*.

serves 4

1kg (2lb 4oz) shelled borlotti beans

3 cloves of garlic, crushed

salt and black pepper

4 plum tomatoes, roughly chopped

bunch of sage

10 tbsp olive oil

4 pork chops

100g (3½oz) butter

600ml (1 pint) milk

1 lemon, cut into wedges, to serve

Preheat the oven to 180°C/350°F/gas mark 4.

Put the beans in an ovenproof dish. Sprinkle over the garlic and season to taste. Add the tomatoes.

Pour in enough water to leave the top layer of beans just showing through. Scatter the sage leaves on top of the beans and pour over 6 tbsp of the olive oil. Bake for 50 minutes.

After 25 minutes, prepare the chops by cutting 2 slashes through the fat up to the meat. Heat the remaining oil and the butter in a frying pan and brown the chops on both sides.

Pour the milk over the chops to half-fill the pan. Cover with a lid and bring to simmering point, then cook on a low heat for 15 minutes. Rest the meat in the liquor with the lid on for 5 minutes.

Remove the beans from the oven, discard the sage leaves and set aside a fifth of the beans. Mash the rest. Put the whole ones back on top and serve with the pork chops and, if you wish, a wedge of lemon.

beetroot

When it comes to beetroot, my moment of clarity
came over lunch at the veg-loving River Café.
Having been subjected to pickled beetroot from
a jar as a child, I wasn't expecting great things when
I was served roasted beetroot alongside two of my
favourite dishes: *carpaccio* and creamed horseradish.
Intending to push the beets to one side, I took an
exploratory slice. If I had been given a whole
bowlful, I would have eaten it. I have been a
beetroot convert ever since. Thank you Ruth Rogers
and Rose Gray.

I am 40 years old now – although my mum says I still look like a young Elvis – and, if you're about the same age as me, your first memories of beetroot will almost certainly be as horrendous as mine. Beetroot was awful; it came out of a jar of vinegar. I went to my nan's for tea every Sunday, and every week I would undergo the ordeal of beetroot from a jar.

In fact, salads all round were a pretty dreary affair in the 1960s and early 1970s. They were composed of iceberg, celery, tomatoes and cucumber. How uninspiring is that? Then, to make matters worse, pickled beetroot was added, smothering the whole ensemble with blood-coloured vinegar. Years of this taste-bud abuse made me mistrust the poor old beetroot so. I was fortunate in having that moment of clarity.

The beetroot is a relative of the chard, and they both make my list of top vegetables, although neither appears to be that popular. I am convinced that my childhood beetroot horror story is shared by countless other unfortunates, and that's why beetroot isn't used more often. The other reason could be that it stains everything – if you don't scrub like a thing possessed, you can end up red-handed for weeks!

types of beetroot

Beetroots are grouped according to shape, and most of the beetroot you buy will be **globe** or **round beetroot**. Within this category come **baby beetroot**, much loved by chefs and restaurateurs because it's little and looks pretty on your plate. Also, because it's smaller, it takes less time to cook. Generally, depending on age, they will be sweeter than your average beetroot.

You have to trust me here and I promise you I haven't been at the cooking sherry, but I was amazed when I first laid eyes on a **chioggia beetroot**. Developed and named after the Italian town of Chioggia, this stunning beet has white spirals running through it. Sliced thinly on a mandolin, it looks like someone has swirled cream into a bowl of bortsch. Unfortunately, when it's cooked, the whole thing goes pink.

Golden beetroot is incredibly pretty – round and canary yellow. I would like to say it's sweeter than the red beetroot – it is in theory – but only if you are eating two beets of the same age. I love them, but they are a rare commodity.

Cheltenham beet is the same shape as a parsnip or carrot. It has the softest flesh of any beetroot I've ever tasted – even softer than baby beet. It's much bigger than

jan	feb	mar	apr	may	jun	jul	aug	sep	oct	nov	dec

normal beets and experience tells us it should be tougher, but it isn't – it's more tender. Clever old Cheltenham.

a few facts about beetroot

All beetroots are descended from the sea beet, which grows wild along the coasts of the Mediterranean and Atlantic. There is evidence that edible roots were being eaten along these coastlines from 300BC.

It is surprising that golden beetroot is now such a rarity and so highly prized. If you asked anybody to describe a beetroot, it would most certainly be red or purple. However, the first beetroot seen in Europe was probably of the golden variety and it is unlikely these beets were round – they would have resembled a parsnip or a carrot in shape. Red beets probably made their way to Britain in the 17th century. The first record we have of this is John Evelyn's recipe for sliced boiled beets, published in 1699.

Beetroots were first cultivated for their leaves. It was a long while before anybody important got hungry enough to eat the dirty root and record it for posterity. Many believe that the roots were first farmed by Romans in the Christian era. Certainly, right up until the Tudor period, people referred to them as Roman beets. That name probably didn't survive the Henrician Reformation. Still, I can't imagine the Pope being that bothered, can you? He was probably more concerned about his churches being looted than the name of a red root veg being changed. I suspect he'd have been even less bothered if he'd known that centuries later someone was to put it in a jar with vinegar.

buying beetroot

The most important things to look at are the leaves and stems. If the leaves are bright and the stems are firm and erect, you have a very happy beetroot. If you are lucky enough to find a beet in this condition, you know it has only just been picked. I don't mind limp stems and drooping leaves; the beetroot will still be very fresh. However, supermarkets hardly ever sell beetroot with the leaf and stem intact. The leaf deteriorates far more quickly than the rest of the plant. If you can't find beetroot with leaves, try to buy your beet with a little stem attached to the root. Don't worry, though, if you can't find either – just make sure the beet isn't broken or bleeding. Squeeze it between your fingers; it shouldn't give an inch and the skin shouldn't wrinkle.

storing beetroot

The leaves and roots will last in the refrigerator for up to 3 days. The roots, kept in a cool, dark place, will last for up to 10 days.

raw beetroot

Peel the beetroot and cut off the stems and root tip. Thinly slice it on a mandolin or grate it.

Try with: salad.

boiling beetroot

Cut off the root tips, leaves and stem (leave a little stem sticking out or else the beetroot will bleed). Bring a large pan of salted water to the boil. Add the beetroot and simmer, lid off, for 30 minutes, depending on the size of your beetroot, until a fork passes through easily. Drain, cool a little, then peel and season.

Try with: ham and mustard.

mashing beetroot

Follow the instructions for boiling beetroot. After draining, mash the beetroot with 15g (1/2oz) butter per 100g (3 1/2oz) beetroot. Add freshly ground black pepper to taste.

Try with: goat's cheese.

roasting beetroot

Preheat the oven to 200°C/400°F/gas mark 6. Cut off the root tips, leaves and stem (leave a little stem sticking out or else the beetroot will bleed). Peel and halve or quarter them, if on the large side, and wrap in kitchen foil. Cook for 20–40 minutes, depending on size, until soft.

Try with: white meat.

baby beetroot and roast pork loin with mustard sauce

The neutral colours of the pork and sauce really highlight the deep crimson of the beets, and the slight acidity of the beets complements the pork well. The sauce and beets on their own would be good enough, but not for a big ugly carnivore like me.

serves 4

1kg (2lb 4oz) pork loin

vegetable oil

400g (14oz) baby beetroots, trimmed

2 tbsp Dijon mustard

1 tbsp English mustard

8 tbsp mayonnaise

25g (1oz) gherkins, chopped

1 tbsp white wine vinegar

Preheat the oven to 190°C/375°F/gas mark 5.

Rub the pork all over with vegetable oil. Place it in a roasting dish and cover with foil. Roast for 1 hour 10 minutes, until cooked through, then allow it to rest for 15 minutes.

After 50 minutes cooking, bring a pan of salted water to the boil and add the beetroots. Simmer for 30 minutes. Drain and peel.

Meanwhile, mix together the mustards, mayonnaise, gherkins and vinegar. Serve the beetroots with the sauce alongside the pork.

beetroot and mackerel salad

Beetroot has a wonderfully soothing influence on oily fish. This dish is no exception.

serves 4

450g (1lb) baby beetroots, peeled

12 cloves of garlic, unpeeled

3 tbsp vegetable oil

salt and black pepper

2 large mackerel fillets, skinned

2 tbsp plain flour

pinch of cayenne pepper

25g (1oz) butter

125g (4½oz) salad leaves, preferably frisée and red chard

1 tsp chopped chives

1 tsp chopped parsley

for the dressing

4 tbsp extra virgin olive oil

1 tbsp lemon juice

1 tbsp creamed horseradish

Preheat the oven to 200°C/400°F/gas mark 6. Halve the beetroots, depending on their size, then trim, leaving a little stalk intact. Put them in a baking dish with the garlic, pour over the vegetable oil and season. Cover with foil and roast for 20–40 minutes, depending on size. Remove the foil and cook for another 15–30 minutes, until tender.

At the point of removing the foil, cook the fish. Run your fingers along it to check for and remove bones. Cut the flesh into bite-size chunks. Season the flour with salt, black pepper and cayenne. Dip the fish into the flour to give a light coating.

Melt the butter in a frying pan over a medium heat, then fry the fish for about 1 minute on each side.

For the dressing, whisk the olive oil, lemon juice and horseradish together and season. Arrange the salad leaves and herbs on a plate. Add the mackerel and beetroot and drizzle with dressing.

bortsch

There are as many bortsch recipes as there are villages in Eastern Europe. I have tried scores of them, and this recipe is the best – taken from a Polish friend of my mate and ex-wife, Denise.

serves 4

2 tbsp sunflower oil

50g (1¾oz) butter

1 onion, diced

1 carrot, diced

1 potato, diced

2 cloves of garlic, crushed

500g (1lb 2oz) beetroots, peeled and diced

1 tbsp caster sugar

850ml (1½ pints) chicken stock

4 tbsp soured cream

a few sprigs of dill

Heat the oil and butter in a pan over a low heat. Add the onion, carrot, potato and garlic, and cook until soft, about 15 minutes.

Add the beetroot and sugar, and cook for another 4 minutes.

Pour in the chicken stock, bring to the boil and simmer for 1 hour.

Blitz with a hand-held blender or in a food processor, then push through a sieve.

Serve in bowls with a dollop of soured cream in the middle and dill scattered on top.

beetroot leaf and goat's cheese tart

I love cooks who use the beet stalks and leaves. Goat's cheese can leave your palate very dry, and the beet stalk and leaf give a nice juiciness after the first crunch.

serves 4

salt and black pepper

250g (9oz) beet leaves and stalks, chopped

25g (1oz) butter, plus extra for greasing

375g (13oz) ready-rolled puff pastry

150g (5½oz) soft goat's cheese, crumbled

1 tbsp oregano leaves

olive oil, for drizzling

1 egg, beaten

Preheat the oven to 220°C/425°F/gas mark 7.

Bring a large pan of salted water to the boil. Drop in the chopped leaves and stalks and blanch for 2 minutes. Drain well.

Melt the butter in a frying pan over a medium heat and, when hot, add the leaves and stalks. Sauté for 3–4 minutes, until excess liquid has boiled away. Season and leave to cool.

Lightly grease a baking tray and line with the pastry. With a sharp knife, draw a line around the pastry about 2–3cm (¾–1¼ inches) inside the edge, but do not cut through.

Spread the cooled beet leaves and stalks within the cut line. Cover with crumbled goat's cheese, oregano and a drizzle of olive oil, then brush the edges with beaten egg. Bake for 20–25 minutes, until golden and risen. Serve immediately.

bok choi and pak choi

Bok choi and pak choi are Chinese in origin.
The names alone conjure up images of big, winding
walls and yellow rivers. Consequently, people tend
to only use them when cooking with a wok or when
preparing an Asian meal. This is a terrible shame.
The neutral flavour of bok choi means that it sits
happily with virtually any plate of food. I like to
have it instead of cabbage with a Sunday roast.
The crunch and juice released is a refreshing contrast
to sticky gravy, as indeed a well-cooked cabbage
should be, but with bok choi you don't get strong
green cabbage flavour.

The major problem with bok choi and pak choi is identification. I have never known such confusion over a vegetable. I must confess that when I started working in the veg trade in the early 1990s, I was confused. These veg have since risen in popularity in London, probably thanks to the many Antipodean chefs who are filling the capital's kitchens. Their home market is, to a large extent, Asia, and for their Asian style of cooking they insist on quality bok choi and pak choi. In those early days, I would receive requests for both of them, and I wouldn't have a clue which was which. I ended up referring to them as quietly as I could as 'uk choi', hoping no one would know whether I was saying bok or pak. To make matters worse, some people refer to them both as Chinese cabbage. Oh, my aching head!

In fact, it's as simple as this: pak choi has a white stem and a green leaf; bok choi is green all over. There is no difference in the texture or flavour of the two, it's simply a question of aesthetics or what you can lay your hands on.

Bok choi and pak choi grow perfectly well in Britain. In fact, at the height of the season they can take as little as 5 weeks from seed to harvesting. My one tip with this vegetable is to wash it well, very much like celery, as the dirt gets into places that other veg don't have.

a few facts about bok choi and pak choi

Bok choi is a brassica, which makes it a member of the cabbage family. If you have never used it, don't be under any illusion; it tastes as much like a green cabbage as your average penguin. Botanists also tell us that it's closely related to the turnip. Makes you wonder, doesn't it? How can bok choi be related to a turnip?

buying bok choi and pak choi

Brown spots are not a problem, and neither is yellowing of the leaf around the edge. In fact, most choi you buy will have a slight yellowing. But if more than the edge is yellowing, this is ageing. The stem should be crisp and the leaves should be upright and not drooping. A lot of shops sell great big stuff, but I would shy away from anything over 15cm (6 inches) long. I do grow baby bok choi about 6cm (2½ inches) long for a London restaurant, but you are unlikely to get your hands on anything like this unless you grow it yourself.

jan	feb	mar	apr	may	jun	jul	aug	sep	oct	nov	dec

storing bok choi and pak choi

Both will keep in the refrigerator for up to 5 days, depending on how fresh they were when you bought them. I would store supermarket varieties for 3 days at the very most, though.

boiling bok choi and pak choi

Wash the choi thoroughly – look for any grit or insects between the leaves. Don't trim or cut it. Bring a large pan of salted water to the boil and once you have a good rolling boil, add the choi. Boil, lid off, for 3 minutes. Drain in a colander.

Try with: any meat or fish.

steaming bok choi and pak choi

Wash the choi thoroughly. Cut it in half and put the halves in a sieve. Bring a lidded pan of salted water to the boil and wait for a good amount of steam to build up before adding the choi. Sit the sieve over the pan of boiling water – ensure it does not touch the water – and cover with the lid. Steam for 5 minutes.

Try with: any meat or fish.

stir-frying bok choi and pak choi

Wash the choi thoroughly, then rip layers from it, one small stalk at a time, and drain well. In a wok, heat 2 tbsp of vegetable oil for every 100g (3½oz) choi. When hot, add the choi and cook over a high heat, stirring continuously, for 3 minutes.

Try with: virtually anything you want to chuck in the wok.

spicy bok choi and chicken stir-fry

I use two types of chilli: the fierce birdseye for heat; and the big ones for colour. I'm not normally into making food look good for the sake of it, but indulge me here.

serves 4

bunch of coriander

2 chicken breasts

6 tbsp sesame oil

4 cloves of garlic, crushed

4 heads of bok or pak choi, quartered

2 birdseye chillies, thinly sliced (keep the seeds)

6 tbsp dark soy sauce

1 big, mild red chilli, deseeded, pith removed and thinly sliced

freshly boiled rice, to serve

Pick the leaves from the coriander and slice the chicken into strips no more than 5mm ($\frac{1}{4}$ inch) thick and 4cm ($1\frac{1}{2}$ inch) long, removing any fat or sinew.

Heat the sesame oil in a wok over a high heat. Drop in the garlic, cook for 30 seconds, then add the chicken, stirring all the time.

When the chicken is coloured, add the bok choi and birdseye chillies and seeds. Pour in the soy and keep stirring.

After 3 minutes, add the mild chilli and cook for 2 minute more, stirring all the time.

Scatter over the coriander leaves and serve with boiled rice.

bok choi with fish and red pepper sauce

It's really unfortunate that people only think of bok choi as an Asian ingredient. Its crunch, unassuming flavour and juiciness makes it a match for any fish, meat or vegetable.

serves 4

1 large red pepper, cored, deseeded and quartered

150g (5$\frac{1}{2}$oz) spicy tomato salsa (see page 135)

80g (2$\frac{3}{4}$oz) butter

3 tbsp vegetable stock

4 heads of bok or pak choi, halved

4 x 150g (5$\frac{1}{2}$oz) pieces of firm, filleted white fish such as haddock, skinned

salt and black pepper

plain flour, for dusting

1 tbsp vegetable oil

Lay the pepper quarters, skin-side up, on a grill tray and grill under a high heat, until the skins are black all over. Put the peppers in a bowl, cover with clingfilm and leave to cool. When cool, peel off the skins and chop the flesh finely. Mix the pepper with the salsa, then cover and set aside.

Melt half the butter with the stock in a large pan over a high heat. Add the bok choi, cover and cook for 4–5 minutes, shaking the pan occasionally to prevent sticking and to ensure even cooking.

Meanwhile, coat the fish lightly with seasoned flour. Melt the remaining butter with the vegetable oil in a large frying pan over a medium heat. When the butter stops foaming, put the fish in the pan, serving-side down. Fry for a couple of minutes, then carefully turn over. When almost cooked, take the pan off the heat.

Put two bits of the steamed bok choi on a plate, top with the fish, and serve with the red pepper sauce on the side.

broccoli

There are three main types of broccoli. The one with the thick stem and big clustery heads is calabrese. The one with thinner stems and a few sprouts is sprouting. And now we have tenderstem, which has a thin, main stem with a head on the end. Broccoli is a brassica, which means it's part of the cabbage family. It closely resembles cauliflower, which is also part of the cabbage family. The green bushy heads you see are flower buds that have started to grow, and stopped – another thing broccoli has in common with cauliflower.

types of broccoli

Calabrese is the broccoli we most recognize, which is bizarre as the sprouting type is by far the oldest, and in my view the best, variety. Calabrese comes from southern Italy and is named after the region it originates from, Calabria. Personally, I don't want that much flowering head; I don't like its texture and the stem is far too thick to eat. In desperation, I've tried slicing the stem into discs, blanching it and frying it like a chip. Still, calabrese continues to outsell the other broccolis, so you guys must know something I don't.

Sprouting is what I want – thin, tender stems releasing light broccoli flavour with every bite, and sparse little sprouts, dense and brush-like in appearance. Unlike calabrese, which is mostly about the head, sprouting broccoli is mostly about the stem.

Tenderstem is a beautiful little vegetable and a relative newcomer. It resembles sprouting broccoli more than it does calabrese in that it is all about the stem. It does have one head at the end of each stem, unlike the sprouting, which, as its name suggests, can sprout many. I've sampled this baby a number of times, and have yet to find a stem that isn't perfectly soft and delicious.

a few facts about broccoli

The earliest archaeological evidence of cultivation is not restricted to Egypt, where so much early evidence of vegetable farming comes from. There is evidence of broccoli growth in what are now Iraq and Syria. And you could fall over the amount of written evidence throughout classical Greece and Rome.

Broccoli is supposed to have arrived in Italy from Crete or Cyprus. It spread to the rest of Europe from Italy. Broccoli was still referred to in England as 'Italian asparagus' as late as the 18th century. Catherine de Medici, that famous gastronome and slayer of Protestants, is credited with introducing broccoli to France from Italy.

sprouting broccoli

| jan | feb | mar | apr | may | jun | jul | aug | sep | oct | nov | dec |

calabrese broccoli

| jan | feb | mar | apr | may | jun | jul | aug | sep | oct | nov | dec |

buying broccoli

With calabrese, the broccoli heads should be tight and dark green to grey-blue. Any yellowing is a sure sign of deterioration and age. With thinner or sprouting broccoli, hold the stem at the base and make sure it stands erect without drooping.

storing broccoli

Even the freshest broccoli will only last for 3 days in the fridge.

raw calabrese broccoli

Lightly peel the stems, then cut them into very thin slices and serve in salads.
Try with: lemon juice and seasoning.

boiling calabrese broccoli florets

Find where the small broccoli branches meet the thick stem and cut the stem off at this point. Break the small branches into florets. Bring a large pan of salted water to the boil. You need a good rolling boil when you add the broccoli – the faster it reboils after green vegetables are added, the more colour is sealed in. Boil the broccoli for 3 minutes with the lid off. Drain in a colander and give it a good shake. Alternatively, boil for just 2 minutes, then toss in a pan with melted butter for 30 seconds.
Try with: any meat or fish.

boiling calabrese broccoli stems

Lightly peel the broccoli stems, then cut them into pound-coin-thick slices. Bring a large pan of salted water to the boil and once you have a good rolling boil, add the stems and boil for 2 minutes with the lid off. Drain in a colander.
Try with: hot, melted butter and plenty of freshly ground black pepper.

calabrese broccoli cooked in cream

Find where the small broccoli branches meet the thick stem and cut the stem off at this point. Break the small branches into florets. Bring a large pan of salted water to the boil and once you have a good rolling boil, add the broccoli and boil for 2 minutes with the lid off. Drain in a colander and give it a good shake. In a large pan, heat 2 tbsp of double cream for every 100g (3 1/2oz) of broccoli. Add the broccoli and stir for 1 minute. Serve immediately.
Try with: white fish or white meat.

steaming calabrese broccoli

Find where the small broccoli branches meet the thick stem and cut the stem off at this point. Break the small branches into florets, then put the florets in a sieve. Bring a pan of salted water to the boil and wait for a good amount of steam to build up before adding the broccoli. Sit the sieve over the pan of boiling water – ensure it does not touch the water – and cover with a lid. Cook for 6 minutes.
Try with: any meat or fish.

stir-frying calabrese broccoli

Find where the small broccoli branches meet the thick stem and cut the stem off at this point. Break the small branches into very small florets. Use 1 tbsp of sunflower oil for every 250g (9oz) of broccoli. Heat the oil in a wok until very hot. Add the broccoli, being careful not to overload the pan, and toss and stir with a wooden spoon. If the crackle in pan is very loud, the heat is too high. Add 2 pinches each of salt and sugar. Cook for 3 minutes and serve immediately.
Try with: stir-fried chicken or red peppers.

boiling sprouting broccoli

Trim the ends off the broccoli. Bring a large pan of salted water to the boil and once you have a good rolling boil, add the broccoli and boil, lid off, for 2 minutes. The broccoli should retain a slight crunch. Drain.
Try with: melted butter.

steaming sprouting broccoli

Trim the ends off the broccoli. Melt a large knob of butter in a large pan and heat with 2–3 tbsp of vegetable or chicken stock over a high heat. As soon as this reaches a boil, add the broccoli and cover. Cook for 4–5 minutes, shaking the pan occasionally to prevent sticking.
Try with: slices of lemon.

broccoli, cheese and haddock bake

Nothing beats this on a rainy autumn evening. The richly satisfying sauce combines with the succulence of the fish perfectly, and its velvety texture is an exquisite match for the crunchy broccoli.

serves 4

juice of ¹/₂ lemon

2 x 150g (5¹/₂oz) pieces of filleted haddock, skinned

salt and black pepper

50g (1³/₄oz) butter, plus extra for greasing

50g (1³/₄oz) plain flour

450ml (16fl oz) full-fat milk

1 tsp Dijon mustard

50g (1³/₄oz) Cheddar, grated

3 tbsp crème fraîche

400g (14oz) calabrese broccoli, cut into medium florets

Preheat the oven to 200°C/400°F/gas mark 6. Butter a gratin dish.

Squeeze a little lemon juice over the haddock and season. Set aside.

Melt the butter in a pan over a medium heat. Add the flour and cook, stirring, for a couple of minutes. Gradually pour in the milk, whisking until smooth. Simmer for 5 minutes, stirring all the time, then add the mustard, salt and pepper, cheese and crème fraîche and stir to combine. Remove from the heat and set aside.

Bring a large pan of salted water to the boil. Drop in the broccoli and boil for 3 minutes, then drain.

Put the broccoli in a buttered gratin dish. Place the haddock on top of the broccoli, then pour the cheese sauce over the top.

Bake for 20-30 minutes, until brown and bubbling and the haddock is cooked through.

sprouting broccoli with hollandaise and anchovies

The crunch of good broccoli and the intensity of the anchovies all covered in the sticky citron of hollandaise – what a great combination. Heaven!

serves 4

salt and black pepper

500g (1lb 2oz) sprouting broccoli, trimmed

2 egg yolks

1 tbsp Dijon mustard

juice of ¹/₂ lemon

125g (4¹/₂oz) butter, melted

5 anchovy fillets, chopped

Bring a large pan of salted water to the boil. Add the broccoli and boil for 4 minutes, lid off. Drain in a colander.

Meanwhile, whisk the yolks, mustard and lemon juice together until doubled in size. Gradually pour in the melted butter, whisking all the time.

Arrange the broccoli on plates, pour over the hollandaise sauce and scatter the anchovies on top. Grind over a generous helping of black pepper.

broccoli and cauliflower gratin

I have a fondness for this dish. It's the combination of Cheddar, yoghurt and mustard as a topping that I find quite irresistible.

serves 4

250g (9oz) cauliflower

250g (9oz) calabrese broccoli

150g (5¹/₂oz) Greek yoghurt

80g (2³/₄oz) Cheddar, grated

1 tsp Dijon mustard

salt and black pepper

25g (1oz) butter

2 tbsp fresh breadcrumbs

Cut the cauliflower and broccoli into florets of an equal size. Bring a large pan of salted water to the boil. Add the vegetables and boil, lid off, for 3 minutes. Drain and place in a heatproof dish.

Mix together the yoghurt, Cheddar and mustard, season and spoon over the veg. Dot with bits of butter, then scatter with the fresh breadcrumbs.

Grill under a medium heat until golden brown – about 2 minutes.

Brussels sprouts

It's a Christmas veg, isn't it, the Brussels sprout?
Well, if not Christmas, then certainly winter.
I've seen sprouts on sale in supermarkets in early
October, flown in from somewhere ridiculous.
Sprouts want frost; the first frost livens them up,
that's why they're a winter veg. The sprout is an
acquired taste. I mean, flavour-wise it's no shrinking
violet – nobody could accuse it of subtlety. And that
taste is not everyone's cup of tea. As you get older,
your taste buds learn to appreciate bitter flavours,
but I detested sprouts as a child; I found them
seriously strong and bitter.

I would try to eat a sprout, slicing off bits and mixing it in with potato, but my mother would ruin it – if I managed it, there would be 2 on the plate at the next meal time. And if I managed to eat these 2, the next time I'd get 3. But as I say, age brings change, and I now appreciate the strength and contrast a sprout delivers. Some kids will eat them, though. I'm the eldest of 3 brothers, and I remember my middle brother, Biffo, climbing on to the kitchen table, crawling over to me and stuffing my sprout whole into his mouth. He had the same expression I'd expect from a hamster trying to swallow a tennis ball! I really enjoy the combination of sprouts sweetened with chestnuts. Why do we only eat it at Christmas? It's a marriage made in heaven!

Brussels sprout tops

As long as there have been sprouts, there have been the tops of sprouts. These are small, soft-leaved, round but flattish little cabbages. Their texture is similar to that of spring greens, although their shape is more saucer-like. Restaurant chefs, always on the lookout for something new, started asking for sprout tops 5 or 6 years ago, and they have caught on. They're a cross between a sprout and a cabbage and you prepare and cook them in the same way as you would a spring green.

a few facts about Brussels sprouts

The sprout is obviously a brassica, but it's anybody's guess when somebody mutated it from its original cabbage. I believe sprouts originated in Belgium, where they were sold in markets as early as the 13th century (they didn't appear in England or France until the end of the 18th century). But most Belgians believe sprouts to be Italian in origin. We know that sprouts were mentioned in Belgian market regulations in 1213. The earliest French record I can find is an order for a wedding feast of the Burgundian court in the 15th century. We have no English recipes until the 19th century.

buying and storing Brussels sprouts

Sprouts can be a deep dark or a lighter green, but make sure there is no yellowing on the edge of the leaf. They should be dry; if you scrunch them together they should squeak. The benefit of buying sprouts on a stem is that they remain sweeter. On or off the stem, they won't last longer than 3 days, but they do freeze well.

jan	feb	mar	apr	may	jun	jul	aug	sep	oct	nov	dec

preparing Brussels sprouts

Wash each sprout and trim the base. Do not cut a cross at the base; it's better to cut larger sprouts in half lengthways and cook as normal.

boiling Brussels sprouts

Bring a pan of salted water to the boil. Drop in the sprouts and boil, lid off, for 3–4 minutes. They should retain some bite. Drain and serve with a knob of butter.
Try with: a stew.

puréeing Brussels sprouts

Bring a pan of salted water to the boil. Drop in the sprouts and boil, lid off, for 3–4 minutes. Drain, then rub through a sieve. Put the sprouts back in the pan over a low heat. Add a knob of butter and a little single cream and stir until a purée is formed.
Try with: fish.

steaming Brussels sprouts

Melt a large knob of butter in a pan over a medium heat. Add 2 tbsp of vegetable or chicken stock per 100g (3½oz) of sprouts. Add the sprouts, cover and cook for 4–5 minutes, shaking the pan often to ensure even cooking.
Try with: liver.

stir-frying Brussels sprouts

Cut the sprouts into halves. Bring a pan of salted water to the boil. Drop in the sprouts and boil, lid off, for 1 minute. Drain. Heat 1 tbsp vegetable oil and a knob of butter per 100g (3½oz) sprouts in a wok. Fry the sprouts for 2 minutes. If you want, fry finely chopped onions and garlic with grated ginger before adding the par-boiled sprouts.
Try with: lamb chops.

steaming Brussels tops

Sprout tops can be treated in the same way as any spring or winter green. Wash and trim the veg. Roll up the leaves and shred quite finely. Melt a large knob of butter in a pan over a medium heat. Add 2 tbsp of vegetable or chicken stock per 100g (3½oz) veg, then add the sprout tops. Cook, lid on, for 3–4 minutes, shaking the pan often.
Try with: a fish pie.

bubble and squeak

Everyone, it seems, loves bubble and squeak. Traditionally the preserve of leftovers, this recipe uses good fresh sprouts or cabbage.

serves 4

90g (3¼oz) butter

1 large onion, finely chopped

900g (2lb) potatoes, boiled and mashed

450g (1lb) freshly cooked sprouts or cabbage, finely sliced

salt and black pepper

Melt 60g (2¼oz) of the butter in a frying pan over a medium heat and cook the onion for about 5 minutes, until softened.

Put the mashed potatoes in a large bowl with the sprouts or cabbage. Mix together with the onions and season well, especially with pepper.

Melt the remaining butter in a large frying pan over a medium heat. Add the potato mixture and fry until it is brown on the bottom. Using a fish slice, turn the bubble and squeak over in as few bits as possible. I do this at least twice, until it is very brown and crispy. Serve topped with a fried egg if you wish.

sprout top and Stilton soup

This comes pretty near to being my favourite ever soup. Bursting with good veg and then rich cheese on top, dishes like this remind me that there is a great architect of the universe looking after our wellbeing.

serves 4

25g (1oz) butter

110g (3¾oz) rindless streaky bacon, cut into small strips

1 onion, finely chopped

2 leeks, roughly chopped

2 carrots, roughly chopped

2 potatoes, cut into 2.5cm (1 inch) dice

250ml (9fl oz) vegetable stock, to cover

salt and black pepper

1 sprout top, finely shredded

110g (3¾oz) Stilton cheese

Melt the butter in a large pan over a medium heat. Fry the bacon very lightly for about 5 minutes. Add the onion, leeks, carrots and potatoes, and sweat for 10 minutes.

Pour in enough stock to cover and season with salt and pepper. Cover and simmer for 20 minutes.

Add the shredded sprout tops and continue to simmer, lid on, for 10–15 minutes.

Check the seasoning and, just before serving, crumble the cheese into the soup.

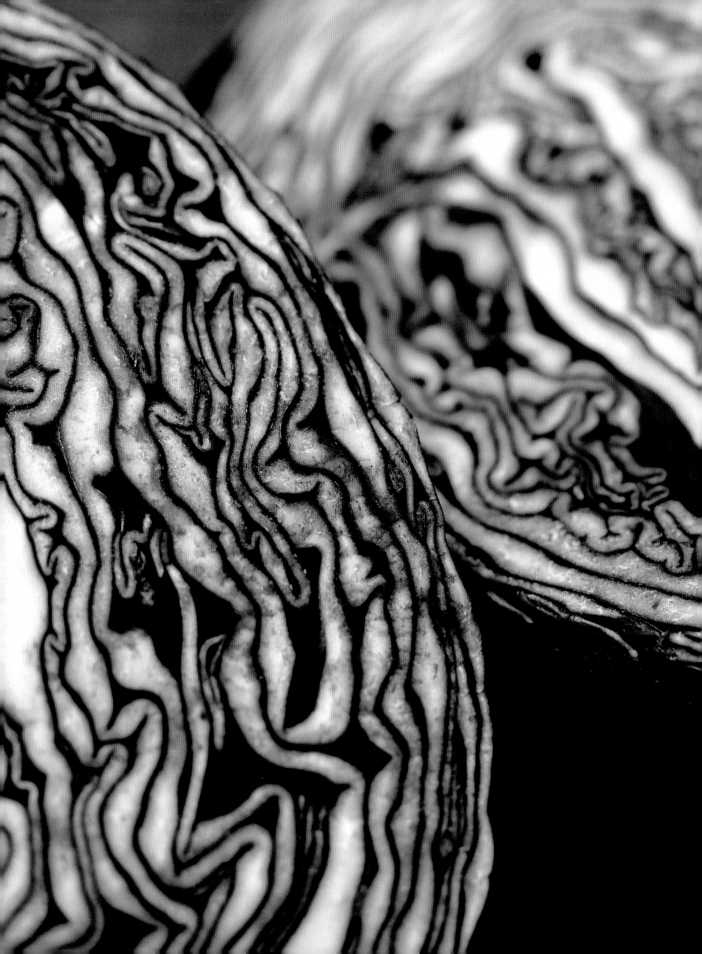

cabbage

I used to detest cabbage as a child, yet I love it now. Maybe it's because I cook my own and I cook it gently. It looks so fantastic, dark green paling to white, on a plate with gravy all over it or butter melting on top. I feel that when I'm eating it I'm doing myself good. It has a crunch, a deep flavour and gives juice all at the same time. Green cabbage floating in stews, swimming in soups or with roast meats and potatoes is a joy. Even cutting through a green cabbage lightens my heart. It's a big boy's vegetable: you rip off big leaves and you need a big knife and a big pot. Yes, I'm fond of cabbage.

I use white cabbage in the same way as green, and it is perfect in coleslaw. Who doesn't like coleslaw? Red cabbage is the ideal accompaniment for game and all that malarkey and marries up with pork extremely well. The only problem is that it's often served with apple, and I don't want my cabbage to be sweet. Also, although when raw red cabbage glows a regal purple, when cooked it goes a grey-pink and stains not only the plate, but everything else it touches. Only puddings should be pink.

The cabbage is one of the only vegetables that will stand up to a harsh winter frost. It just sits there in the ground all winter, waiting for someone to come along and crop it. It's like the earth is its natural refrigerator.

The cabbage is also extremely good value for money. You buy one, it lasts for ages, and you can do so many things with it. But always cook it gently. The awful smell of boiling cabbage is caused by sulphur from the earth. The cabbage sucks it up, keeps it, and then releases it when we cook it for too long. I think it's the cabbage's defence system; it doesn't want to be boiled and boiled.

types of cabbages

The cabbage is a brassica. Its cousins are broccoli and cauliflower. All of our cabbages stem from the wild sea cabbage, which is still seen along our coastlines. In fact, left alone to go to seed and regrow, all brassicas will revert back to this wild cabbage in an amazingly short period of time.

closed cabbages, including white, red and Savoy

jan	feb	mar	apr	may	jun	jul	aug	sep	oct	nov	dec

spring and winter greens

jan	feb	mar	apr	may	jun	jul	aug	sep	oct	nov	dec

open cabbages, including cavolo nero and kale

jan	feb	mar	apr	may	jun	jul	aug	sep	oct	nov	dec

sea kale

jan	feb	mar	apr	may	jun	jul	aug	sep	oct	nov	dec

There are many varieties of cabbage, all with different cropping times, so it's possible to eat them all year round. In the winter we get the big heavy **red** and **white cabbages** and the fantastically rubbery and wrinkly **Savoy**; in the spring we get the **spring green** or **hispi** with the cone-shaped pointy centre; and in the autumn the **kales** appear. Also, early in the year we get the **January king**, which is a green head with big loose outer leaves that display a fine mixture of red and green; it looks like a green cabbage that someone has thrown red paint over.

Cabbages fall into two main types: headed, like a Savoy or a white cabbage, and those that don't form heads but sprout longer leaves from a stem – i.e the kales. The **cavolo nero**, meaning black cabbage, is a kale. The cavolo is a trendy veg and I don't mind that. What I do mind is the name we use for it. I was thumbing through an old 1970s seed catalogue, and there it was, unmistakeably – an open-headed cabbage, long, wrinkled, almost black, with spear-shaped leaves. Underneath the picture was its name, 'palm-tree cabbage'. This kale has been with us for aeons, but very few of us used it until we discovered that it's a favoured vegetable of the Tuscans, and so renamed it.

a few facts about cabbages

The cabbage was widely used by the ancient Egyptians, Greeks and Romans. It was originally thought that the Romans brought it to Britain, but now historians think it may have been the Saxons.

A lot of vegetables have been credited with all sorts of nonsense, but by far the silliest I have so far encountered is the old Roman belief that eating cabbage is a protection against drunkenness.

Greek mythology has its own explanation for the smell of boiling cabbage. Apparently, Zeus got himself in a bit of a lather trying to explain two conflicting prophecies; the sweat from his brow fell to the ground and formed cabbages, which is why they smell the way they do.

buying cabbages

Check there is no yellowing in the leaf and that the outer leaves are firm and crisp. Turn it over and check the area where the stem has been cut off; this will be wet if the cabbage is very fresh, but as it ages it dries, turns white and gets rough.

storing cabbages

A fresh cabbage will last in the fridge for up to 10 days.

preparing Savoy, green and white cabbages and spring greens

Discard any old or scruffy leaves. Cut the cabbage into quarters through the stalk.
Slice out the hard core in each quarter. Now either chop, dice, slice or shred
the cabbage.

boiling Savoy, green and white cabbages and spring greens

Bring a large pan of salted water to the boil. Add the chopped, diced, sliced or
shredded cabbage and boil until tender, about 4 minutes. Drain well and season.
Try with: pork.

cooking Savoy, green and white cabbages and spring greens in cream

Bring a large pan of salted water to the boil. Add the chopped, diced, sliced or
shredded cabbage and boil until tender, about 4 minutes. Drain well. Put into a clean
pan and add 2 tbsp of double cream for every 250g (9oz) of cabbage. Reheat, adding
10g (¼oz) of butter per 100g (3½oz) of cabbage and lots of pepper.
Try with: mutton.

pan-finishing Savoy, green and white cabbages and spring greens

Bring a large pan of salted water to the boil. Add the chopped, diced, sliced or
shredded cabbage and boil until tender, about 4 minutes. Drain well. Melt 1 tsp butter
in a pan over a medium heat. Add the cabbage, season and cook, stirring, until warm.
Try with: meat stews.

steaming Savoy, green and white cabbages and spring greens

Melt a large knob of butter in a large pan over a high heat. Add 3 tbsp of chicken or
vegetable stock per 100g (3½oz) of cabbage and bring to the boil. Add the chopped,
diced, sliced or shredded cabbage, season well and cover the pan. Cook for 4 minutes,
shaking the pan occasionally to prevent sticking and to ensure even cooking. Stick a
fork in as you go, as all cabbages have different textures.
Try with: different herbs and spices. Dill or fennel seeds work well for me, too.

stir-frying Savoy, green and white cabbages and spring greens
Heat 1 tbsp of vegetable oil in a wok over a high heat. Add 100g (3½oz) of shredded cabbage and stir for 2 minutes, until the cabbage is completely coated with oil. Add 2 tbsp of vegetable or chicken stock. Season, then cook, stirring, for another minute.
Try: crunching some chilli in and having it on its own.

boiling cavolo nero and kale
Cut the hard bottom from the stem and wash the cabbage well. Chop lengthways down, making sure you have 2 symmetrical halves with leaf either side of them. Then cut through the stem at 2.5cm (1 inch) intervals to make small triangular chunks with leaf. Bring a large pan of salted water to the boil. Add the prepared cabbage, season and cook for 5 minutes. Drain.
Try with: borlotti beans.

pan-finishing cavolo nero and kale
Cut the hard bottom from the stem and wash the cabbage well. Chop through the stem, making sure you have leaf either side of it, then cut through the stem at 2.5cm (1 inch) intervals. Bring a large pan of salted water to the boil. Add the prepared cabbage and cook for 5 minutes. Drain well. Melt some butter in a pan over a medium heat and stir in the cooked cavolo nero or kale until warm. Season.
Try with: slices of roast meats.

steaming cavolo nero and kale
Cut the hard bottom from the stem and wash the cabbage well. Chop through the stem, making sure you have leaf either side of it, then cut through the stem at 2.5cm (1 inch) intervals. Melt a large knob of butter in a large pan over a high heat. Add 4 tbsp of chicken or vegetable stock per 100g (3½oz) of cabbage and bring to the boil. Add the leaves, season well and cover the pan. Cook on a high heat for 5 minutes, shaking the pan occasionally to prevent sticking and ensure even cooking.
Try with: lamb chops.

sausage and cabbage layer

Here's one for the winter, and the whole thing should cost you almost nothing! I would serve this with mashed potato and gravy. Pork and cabbage – you know it's a winner.

serves 4

salt and black pepper

800g (1lb 12oz) Savoy, green or white cabbage, thickly sliced

50g (1³/₄oz) butter

400g (14oz) really good sausages, skinned and flattened

Preheat the oven to 150°C/300°F/gas mark 2.

Bring a large pan of salted water to the boil. Add the cabbage and boil for 4 minutes. Drain, cool under a cold tap, and drain again thoroughly.

Grease a lidded casserole dish with half the butter. Cover the base with a third of the cooked cabbage. Arrange half the flattened sausages over the top, then cover with another third of the cabbage. Add the rest of the sausages, then cover with the rest of the cabbage. Remember to season each layer with salt and pepper.

Dot with the remaining butter, cover and cook in the oven for 2 hours. When cooked, the cabbage should be very tender.

crispy seaweed

This is so simple, and my kids scoff it by the handful. I don't know how much you will eat, so cook as much Savoy cabbage as you want.

serves as many as you like

sunflower oil, for deep-frying

Savoy cabbage

salt (1 tsp per 100g/3¹/₂oz cabbage)

sugar (1 tsp per 100g/3¹/₂oz cabbage)

Heat the oil in a large heavy-based pan; it is ready when a bit of cabbage dropped into it sizzles.

Meanwhile, discard the outer leaves of the cabbage. Remove the white stalk from each leaf you use. Roll each leaf into a tight tube and slice very finely.

Deep-fry the cabbage strips in the hot sunflower oil until cooked. Toss with salt and sugar to serve.

stuffed cabbage leaves

This is exactly how I love to eat. Just give me a bowl of mashed potato and lock me in a room with these stuffed cabbage leaves. Cook more than you need, as they make a brilliant midnight snack.

serves 6

1 large Savoy cabbage
salt and black pepper
1 tbsp vegetable oil
25g (1oz) butter
1 large onion, finely chopped
500g (1lb 2oz) lean minced beef
150g (5¹/₂oz) long-grain rice, freshly cooked
1 egg, beaten
2 tbsp finely chopped dill
400g tin chopped tomatoes
250ml (9fl oz) beef stock
1 tbsp cornflour
100ml (3¹/₂fl oz) soured cream
bunch of flat-leaf parsley, roughly chopped, to serve

Preheat the oven to 180°C/350°F/gas mark 4.

Discard any ripped or discoloured outer leaves of the cabbage. Carefully pull off the other leaves individually, without tearing.

Lay the leaves flat and cut away half of the stalk, keeping the leaves intact.

Bring a pan of salted water to the boil. Add the leaves and boil, lid on, for 4 minutes. Drain them in a colander and rinse with cold water. Put the leaves to one side.

Heat the oil and butter together in a pan over a medium heat. Add the onion and fry until soft and golden. Tip into a large bowl.

Add the beef, rice and beaten egg to the onion. Season to taste and add half the dill. Mix together with your hands.

Lay 3–4 cabbage leaves on a flat surface. Depending on the size of your leaf, put 2–3 tbsp of the meat mixture on to each leaf. Roll the leaves up from the stalk end, tucking in the sides as you go.

Place the stuffed leaves in a roasting dish, seam-side down. Continue stuffing until you run out of mixture or leaf.

Mix the tomatoes and beef stock together in a pan and cook over a medium heat for 2 minutes, until warm. Spoon 2 tbsp of this liquid into a cup and mix with the cornflour. Whisk the soured cream and remaining dill into the cornflour, then whisk the whole lot into the pan with the stock in it. Season well and pour over your rolls.

Bake, uncovered, for about 30 minutes. Serve sprinkled with roughly chopped flat-leaf parsley.

red cabbage and pork pot roast

This is simple to prepare and can be left to cook slowly in the oven.

serves 4

salt and black pepper

3 tbsp red wine vinegar

450g (1lb) red cabbage, finely shredded

225g (8oz) cooking apple, peeled, cored and sliced

1 tbsp brown sugar

1 tsp chopped sage

1 tbsp plain flour

700g (1lb 9oz) piece of boneless pork shoulder, rind removed

Preheat the oven to 190°C/375°F/gas mark 5.

Bring a large pan of salted water to the boil. Add 1 tbsp of the vinegar and the cabbage and bring it back to the boil. Remove from the heat immediately and drain the cabbage.

Place the apple and cabbage in a casserole dish just wide enough to hold the pork joint. Add the sugar, remaining vinegar, sage and flour, then stir and season.

Slash the fat side of the pork several times and season. Place on top of the cabbage. Cover with a lid and bake for 1¾ hours, until the pork is tender and cooked through.

Serve slices of pork with the cabbage.

Savoy cabbage and crab coleslaw

I first came across something like this at Christopher's American Bar and Grill in Covent Garden, cooked by Adrian Searing. I believe that Alastair Little was also very taken with it. This is not Adrian's recipe nor Alastair's; it is my attempt to recreate a very good plate of food. I have deliberately omitted amounts for some ingredients. I do feel with the hindsight of experience, that the balance of these flavours is purely a matter of taste.

serves 4

1 Savoy cabbage

salt and black pepper

½ small white cabbage, very finely sliced

1 dressed crab, any size

2 carrots, grated

1 spring onion, trimmed and finely sliced

mayonnaise, to taste

lemon juice, to taste

parsley, finely chopped, to taste

chervil, finely chopped, to taste

Discard any ripped or discoloured outer leaves of the Savoy. Carefully pull off the remaining leaves without tearing them.

Bring a large pan of salted water to the boil. Add the Savoy leaves and boil, lid on, for 4 minutes. Drain and instantly refresh in cold water. Drain well and set aside.

Mix the rest of the ingredients together in a salad bowl, tasting as you go until you get the balance that you like, and season well.

Put a spoonful of the coleslaw on to each Savoy leaf. Roll the leaves up, starting from the stalk end and tucking the sides in as you go. Serve seam-side down.

spring greens, gammon and bean soup

There are some bowls of food that are worth going on a long walk for, and this is one of them. Pig, greens and beans, topped with the reserved heat of paprika.

serves 4

450g (1lb) piece of gammon, soaked in water in the fridge overnight

2 bay leaves

2 onions, finely sliced

2 tsp paprika

675g (1lb 8oz) boiling potatoes, cut into large chunks

225g (8oz) spring greens

410g tin cannellini beans, drained

salt and black pepper

Put the soaked gammon in a large pot with the bay leaves, onions and 1.5 litres (2¾ pints) of cold water. Bring to the boil, then reduce the heat and simmer, lid on, for about 1½ hours.

Drain the gammon, reserving the cooking water. Trim the meat, cutting off the skin, and cut it into cubes of 2.5cm (1 inch). Return to the pot with the reserved cooking water, paprika and potatoes. Cover and simmer for 20 minutes.

Cut away the stalky bits from the greens, then cut them into fine shreds. Add them to the pan with the beans. Season well and simmer, lid off, for 10 minutes.

chilli greens

Take your pick of greens here. You could use kale, Swiss chard, spinach or spring greens.

serves 4

4 tbsp vegetable oil

3 cloves of garlic, crushed

5cm (2 inch) piece ginger, peeled and grated

125g (4½oz) chicken breast, skinned and very finely sliced to no more than 5mm (¼ inch) thick

500g (1lb 2oz) greens, finely chopped

1 red chilli, finely shredded

3 tbsp oyster sauce

1 tbsp brown sugar

2 tsp cornflour mixed with 50ml (2fl oz) water

salt and black pepper

Heat the oil in a wok over a high heat. Add the garlic and ginger and fry for a minute; do not brown. Add the sliced chicken and cook, stirring all the time, for 2–4 minutes.

Add the chopped greens, chilli, oyster sauce, sugar and cornflour and water mixture. Stir and add a further 1 tbsp of water. Fry until the greens are nearly cooked – about 5 minutes. Season and serve straight away.

carrots

The carrot is the most cultivated root vegetable on the planet. Young or baby carrots are tender and taste fantastic cooked simply and served with butter. Slightly older carrots have a more pronounced flavour and are great with sauces or in salads. However, it is as a winter crop that carrots get really interesting; they have a stronger flavour than their early-season counterparts, and can stand up to stews and soups. Compared with most root veg, carrots are wonderfully sweet. During the war, when sugar was in short supply, sweet vegetables such as carrots and parsnips were used for cakes and pastries.

What about the old wives' tale about carrots helping you see in the dark? Well, they're packed with vitamin A, which is essential for good optics, but that's as far as it goes.

types of carrots

Carrots come in many colours: purple, yellow, white, red and orange. And you can find them round in shape. But shape or colour makes no real difference to flavour. I didn't realise until quite recently that wild carrots are everywhere. They have a pretty delicate white flower, that I'm sure most people would recognize instantly, and a tiny, bitter-tasting root. Probably just like me, you've seen them but didn't realise they were carrots. You can get fresh young carrots from March to the end of September, while the winter crops are available from October to February.

a few facts about carrots

Carrot seeds have been found in prehistoric lake dwellings in Switzerland. They were also listed as a plant grown in the royal garden of Babylon in the 8th century BC. Unfortunately, they weren't listed as a veg; they were catalogued with the herbs. Strangely, there is no evidence of carrot-eating by the Greeks or Romans, so cultivation must have continued for the carrot's leaves or seeds to be used as a flavouring.

The earliest written examples we have of people eating carrots as a root are for the dark red or purple carrots. The carrot was carried westwards by the Arabs, and the earliest surviving written evidence of this comes from one Ibn al-Awam, a 12th-century Arab writer, who lived in southern Spain.

Our Tudor ancestors ate carrots, but again there was no sign of an orange one – Queen Elizabeth I would have munched on a yellow or purple variety. They became very trendy in Stuart times; in fact, it became the height of fashion for ladies to pin carrot tops to their hats. How daft is that? Carrots even make an appearance in Shakespeare's *The Merry Wives of Windsor*.

buying carrots

Try to buy carrots with the ferns attached. The ferns are the first bits to rot, so if the fern is intact you know the carrot is fresh. Unfortunately, I have just seen a tasteless slow-rotting Dutch carrot with a slow-rotting fern, so be careful. In fact, be afraid!

| jan | feb | mar | apr | may | jun | jul | aug | sep | oct | nov | dec |

If you can't find carrots with ferns on, watch out for discolouring or sponginess to the touch. A good carrot should be firm, bright and erect.

storing carrots

Keep carrots in a cool, dark place. A decent carrot should last for a week.

preparing baby carrots

The following applies to baby carrots as well as for standard carrots. However, the babies will probably not need peeling and should be kept whole.

raw carrots

Try peeled, grated carrot in salads or as a side dish to accompany all sorts of spicy dishes. They are also good peeled and either eaten whole or sliced lengthways with dips. Try: in salads.

boiling carrots

Peel, top and tail the carrots and cut them into rounds as thick as your little finger. Bring a pan of salted water to the boil. Reduce the heat to a simmer – if the carrots are boiled they may break up during cooking. Simmer for 5 minutes, lid off, then drain in a colander.
Try with: a mustard sauce made from English mustard, cream and pulped-up gherkins.

braising carrots

Preheat the oven to 180°C/350°F/gas mark 4. Peel, top and tail your carrots and cut them in half lengthways. Place them in an ovenproof dish. Add crushed garlic to taste, and a big knob of butter – as much as your courage will allow – then cover with chicken stock. Cover the dish with foil. Bake for 30 minutes. Drain off excess liquid.
Try with: boiled ham.

roasting carrots

Carrots suit roasting well, as the slow caramelization of the cooking really enhances their sweetness. This is my favourite method, especially when the carrots are roasted slowly alongside a joint – I like them when they've fallen apart so much that they have to be eaten with a spoon. Preheat the oven to 200°C/400°F/gas mark 6. Peel and top and tail your carrots. Cut them in half widthways, then cut these halves in half again lengthways. Put the carrots in an ovenproof dish and pour over 1 tbsp of vegetable oil for every 100g (3½oz) of carrots. Add a sprinkle of fresh thyme, cover the dish with foil and bake for 30 minutes. Drain on kitchen towel.

Try with: chicken.

steaming carrots

Peel, top and tail the carrots and cut them into rounds as thick as your little finger. Put the rounds in a sieve. Bring a pan of salted water to the boil and wait for a good amount of steam to build up before adding the carrots. Sit the sieve over the pan of boiling water – ensure it does not touch the water – and cover with a lid. Cook for 7 minutes.

Try with: any roast meat.

carrot and ginger soup

The photographer, Simon, said this recipe was the best carrot and ginger soup he had ever eaten. Can't say fairer than that.

serves 4

1 tbsp vegetable oil

50g (1¾oz) butter

1 onion, finely chopped

1 stalk of celery, sliced

450g (1lb) young carrots, sliced

2 small potatoes, chopped into 2.5cm (1 inch) dice

2 tbsp grated fresh ginger

1 tsp ground ginger

1 litre (1¾ pints) vegetable or chicken stock

200ml (7fl oz) full-fat milk

2–3 leafy celery tops, chopped

salt and black pepper

Heat the oil and 25g (1oz) of the butter in a large pan over a medium heat. Add the onion and fry gently for 5 minutes, until softened but not brown. Add the celery, carrots and potatoes, cover the pan and sweat the vegetables over a medium heat for 10 minutes, stirring once or twice.

Add the fresh and ground ginger, the stock and milk and bring to the boil. Reduce the heat and simmer, lid off, for 15 minutes, until the carrots and potatoes are tender.

Towards the end of the cooking time, melt the remaining butter in a pan and fry the celery tops.

When the soup is ready, whiz until smooth using a hand-held blender. Season well. Serve sprinkled with some of the fried chopped celery tops.

baby carrots with dips

I'm lucky enough to grow carrots with different colours and shapes, so I can serve a variety with these dips. But orange carrots are fine. You really can't go wrong with this dish. These dips taste brilliantly with other veg, too.

serves 6

48 baby carrots with ferns attached

for the mint dip

4 tbsp natural yoghurt

juice of ¹/₂ lemon

] tsp finely chopped mint leaves

black pepper

for the blue cheese dip

4 tbsp blue cheese

4 tbsp double cream

black pepper

for the hot dip

4 tbsp mayonnaise

¹/₂ tbsp tomato purée

1 tbsp tomato ketchup

¹/₂ tsp Worcestershire sauce

1 tsp Tabasco sauce

for the caper dip

1 tbsp finely chopped tarragon

1 tbsp chopped gherkin

1 tbsp chopped capers

Wash and peel the carrots, leaving the ferns on.

For the mint dip, combine all the ingredients in a bowl.

For the blue cheese dip, whisk the cheese until it is creamy. Mix with the cream and black pepper.

For the hot dip, combine all the ingredients in a bowl.

For the caper dip, combine all the ingredients in a bowl.

Serve the carrots with dips on each plate.

carrot cake

Everyone needs a slice of cake with their cup of tea once in a while – it's part of being English. And this cake is a classic.

serves 8

225g (8oz) unsalted butter, softened

225g (8oz) soft light brown sugar

4 eggs, separated

finely grated zest of ½ orange

4 tbsp lemon juice

175g (6oz) self-raising flour

1 tsp baking powder

50g (1¾oz) ground almonds

125g (4½oz) walnut pieces, chopped

350g (12oz) young carrots, peeled and grated

225g (8oz) cream cheese

2 tbsp clear honey

Preheat the oven to 180°C/350°F/gas mark 4. Grease and line the bottom of a 20cm (8 inch) round cake tin.

Using a wooden spoon or in a food processor, cream the butter and sugar together until pale and fluffy. Beat in the egg yolks, orange zest and 3 tbsp of the lemon juice.

Sift in the flour and baking powder, then carefully stir in the ground almonds and 100g (3½oz) of the chopped walnuts.

In a separate bowl, whisk the egg whites until stiff peaks form, then fold them into the mixture along with the grated carrots. Pour the mixture into the prepared tin and make a slight hollow in the centre.

Bake for 1½ hours. Cover the top with kitchen foil after 1 hour if it is browning too quickly. Remove from the oven and leave to cool slightly. Turn out on to a wire rack and remove the lining paper. Leave to cool completely.

Mix together the cream cheese, honey and 1 tbsp lemon juice and use to ice the top of the cake. Scatter with the remaining walnuts.

cauliflower

Cauliflower is a good veg, isn't it? Its whiteness looks so clean and good for you. And it is. The cauliflower is a variety of cabbage in which the flowers have begun to bud but have stopped growing (the white bits of a cauliflower are these buds). It stores nutrients in the thick stems that are under the buds, which would have gone into the flowers if their development hadn't been cut short. So it really is good for you! Cauliflower is more popular in the home than in restaurants, and is particularly well-loved as an accompaniment for a roast dinner.

But the cauliflower is an extremely versatile little brassica. Eaten raw, it adds a freshness and crunch to salads. It makes great soups, is popular as cauliflower cheese, and can stand up to strong flavours, making it ideal for stir-fries and curries.

The cauliflower is closely related to the cabbage. In fact, if you leave cauliflowers to their own devices and don't harvest them, they revert back to being a wild cabbage after about 10 generations.

Back in the 1980s, when *nouvelle cuisine* was at its height, we used to import and sell baby cauliflowers from Paris. I still see them in some supermarkets from time to time. They must cost about £2 each and are definitely not worth the money unless you are desperate for their fancy appearance! If you want a little bit of cauliflower on your plate, break off a floret.

types of cauliflower

Cauliflowers fall into two categories: summer and winter. In the summer, we mostly eat our own home-grown caulis. They are remarkably quick to grow considering their size. One variety, **snowball**, can go from seed to harvest in as little as 50 days.

Along with kohlrabi, **romanesco** – a variety of cauliflower – wins the prize as the weirdest-looking vegetable ever. I suspect that if Martians landed and planted their own vegetables, this is what they would look like. From afar, romanesco looks like a lime green cauliflower, and closer inspection reveals scores of little pyramids. Now, apart from Dairylea spread and Toblerone, I don't know any other triangular food. There are, it's true, a couple of other varieties of green cauliflower, the most successful being **alverda**, but none with pyramids. Those pyramids form the same way as florets on other varieties of cauliflower; they are actually flowers that got no further than the bud stage.

Winter cauliflowers can take a year to grow and you mostly find them in coastal areas, where the frost isn't very severe. Most of the winter caulis we eat are imported from France.

a few facts about cauliflower

No one is sure where the cauliflower originated. Many claim it was brought into southern Europe with the spread and conquests of Islamic Arabs. Cypriots claim it

jan	feb	mar	apr	may	jun	jul	aug	sep	oct	nov	dec

originated in their country – *Larousse Gastronomique* claims it comes from Cyprus. In fact, the original French name for cauliflower is *chou de Chypre* (Cyprus cabbage). The cauliflower was first recorded in England by Gerard in the late 16th century. That's quite late for a vegetable as popular as a cauli. It didn't become widely eaten until the end of the 18th century. I can't think why!

buying cauliflower

Look for cauliflower with leaves curling around the florets. If it is really fresh, the leaves will be bright green. Don't be put off by any little rust spots on the florets and there is no need to look for a whiter-than-white head; yellow is fine, white turning yellow is not.

storing cauliflower

Wrap your cauliflower in clingfilm and keep it in the fridge for up to 3 days.

raw cauliflower

Rip off the big outer leaves of the cauliflower, cut off the stalk, then rip off the remaining leaves. Turn the cauliflower over so that the core is uppermost. Insert a knife into where the florets join the stem, at an angle to the stem, and follow the stem around, cutting through as you do. Break the cauliflower into smaller florets.
Try with: smashed anchovies with extra-virgin olive oil and a squeeze of lemon juice.

boiling cauliflower

Follow the instructions for preparing raw cauliflower. Bring a large pan of salted water to the boil, add the florets and cook, lid off, for about 3 minutes, or until al dente – the size of the florets will determine the length of cooking.
Try with: a pork chop.

puréeing cauliflower

Follow the instructions for preparing raw cauliflower. Bring a large pan of salted water to the boil, and cook the florets for about 6 minutes, or until al dente. Drain, then add 2 tbsp of double cream and 1 tsp of butter for every 100g (3½oz) of cauliflower and purée using a hand-held blender. Season with black pepper.
Try with: roast beef.

steaming cauliflower

Follow the instructions for preparing raw cauliflower. Put the florets in a sieve. Bring a pan of salted water to the boil and wait for a good amount of steam to build up before adding the florets. Sit the sieve over the pan of boiling water – ensure it does not touch the water – and cover with the lid. Cook for 4 minutes.
Try with: Marmite.

cauliflower stems, raw or boiled

Follow the instructions for preparing raw cauliflower. Slice the stem thinly with a mandolin (it can be eaten raw in a salad). Bring a pan of salted water to the boil and boil the slices, lid off, for 2 minutes. Drain, then mix with olive oil and lemon to taste.

roasting romanesco

Treat a romanesco as you would any other variety of cauliflower, but it's nice to keep its shape and colour. Slice it into big chunks and simply roast it with some oil at 180°C/350°F/gas mark 4 for 20 minutes. You may also want to sprinkle on some cheese.

cauliflower cheese

This used to be taught in all home economics classes in school. My advice is to experiment with different cheeses.

serves 4

4 tomatoes
salt and black pepper
450g (1lb) cauliflower, broken into florets
50g (1³/₄oz) butter
75g (2³/₄oz) plain flour
250ml (9fl oz) full-fat milk
1 tbsp English mustard
100ml (3¹/₂fl oz) single cream
75g (2³/₄oz) Double Gloucester cheese, grated
75g (2³/₄oz) mature Cheddar, grated
2 tsp Worcestershire sauce
2 tbsp tomato salsa (see p 135)

Drop the tomatoes into boiling water for 2 minutes. Drain, peel and chop. Preheat the oven to 220°C/425°F/gas mark 7.

Bring a large pan of salted water to the boil. Drop in the cauliflower florets and boil for 3 minutes. Drain well.

Melt the butter in a pan over a medium heat. Add the flour and cook, stirring, for 2 minutes. Gradually pour in the milk, whisking until smooth. Simmer for 5 minutes, stirring all the time, until the sauce thickens. Whisk in the mustard and cream, then most of the cheeses and the Worcestershire sauce. Season with pepper.

Mix the tomatoes and salsa together and place in the bottom of a gratin dish. Cover with the cauliflower, then the sauce. Sprinkle with the remaining cheese and bake for 20 minutes, until brown and bubbling.

cauliflower tempura

This is a great snack. Cauliflower is a subtle fellow, which is why it is usually served as an accompaniment. But with a good batter over it and a coating of tangy mayo, cauli becomes a star.

serves 4

salt

450g (1lb) cauliflower, cut into medium florets

115g (4oz) plain flour

2 eggs, separated

175ml (6fl oz) iced water

vegetable oil, for deep-frying

Bring a large pan of salted water to the boil. Drop in the cauliflower and boil for 2 minutes. Drain in a colander and run under a cold tap. Drain well again and put aside.

Put the flour in a large bowl with a pinch of salt. Whisk the egg yolks and iced water together, then whisk into the flour to make a smooth batter. Beat in 2 tbsp of vegetable oil. In a separate bowl, whisk the egg whites until they form stiff peaks, then fold them into the batter.

In a large heavy-based pan or in a deep-fat fryer, heat the vegetable oil to 190°C/375°F. Test to see if it is hot enough by dropping in a bit of batter; if it sizzles your oil is ready. Dip the cauliflower florets into the batter to coat, then deep-fry them for 2–3 minutes, until golden and puffy. Drain on kitchen towel and continue with the rest of the cauliflower.

Serve with a bowl of aïoli (below) to dip the tempura into.

aïoli

This dip complements many veg, and is a particularly good match for tempura (see above). Recipes for it vary slightly, but this one is my favourite.

6 cloves of garlic, crushed

3 egg yolks

3 tbsp fresh breadcrumbs

$^1/_2$ tsp salt

4 tbsp white wine vinegar

300ml (10fl oz) olive oil

Put the garlic, egg yolks, breadcrumbs, salt and vinegar into a processor. Blitz to a paste and, very slowly, dribble in the olive oil to make a thick sauce. Add 1 tbsp of boiling water at the end and blitz in the processor again.

cauli from the Sam Clarks

The Clarks are lovely people and their restaurant, Moro, is simply superb. They did this recipe when they came on *Veg Talk*. Since then it's been a favourite of mine. Just be careful with the saffron; too much and you will kill the dish.

serves 4

50 strands saffron

75g (2³/₄oz) raisins

salt and white pepper

1 cauliflower, broken into tiny florets (the Clarks use the smallest leaves)

3 tbsp olive oil

1 large onion, finely sliced

5 tbsp pine nuts, toasted

Pour 4 tbsp of boiling water over the saffron in a bowl, then soak the raisins in warm water in a separate bowl.

Bring a pan of salted water to the boil. Boil the cauli, and leaves if using, for 1 minute. Drain, rinse with cold water, and drain again.

Heat the oil in a pan over a low heat. Cook the onion for about 15 minutes, until golden, stirring occasionally. Remove, drain off the oil, and set the onions aside in a bowl. Drain the raisins.

Heat the drained oil to hot then add the cauliflower and leaves if using. Fry, stirring, until you have a bit of colour, about 3 minutes. Add the onion, saffron water, pine nuts and raisins and cook for 3 minutes, until the water has more or less evaporated. Season.

cauliflower soufflés

Soufflés scare most people. Maybe it's because if they go wrong there's nowhere to turn – you just have bowls of sunken stuff. Follow this and I promise it will work every time.

serves 8

50g (1³/₄oz) butter, plus extra for greasing

salt and black pepper

225g (8oz) cauliflower, broken into small florets

3 tbsp plain flour

200ml (7fl oz) full-fat milk

1 tbsp Dijon mustard

100g (3¹/₂oz) Cheddar, grated

¹/₂ green chilli, finely chopped

4 eggs, separated

Preheat the oven to 180°C/350°F/gas mark 4. Grease 8 ramekins.

Bring a large pan of salted water to the boil. Drop in the cauliflower and boil for 3 minutes, until the cauliflower is tender.

Melt the butter in a pan over a medium heat. Stir in the flour and cook. Gradually pour in the milk, whisking until smooth and thick. Simmer for 3 minutes, then add the mustard and season.

Blitz the white sauce in a food processor with the cooked cauli.

Put the cauliflower mixture in a bowl and leave to cool a little. Stir in the grated cheese, chopped chilli and egg yolks.

Whisk the egg whites until stiff, then fold gently into the cauliflower mixture. Spoon into ramekins and bake for 25 minutes, until brown and firm to the touch. Serve immediately.

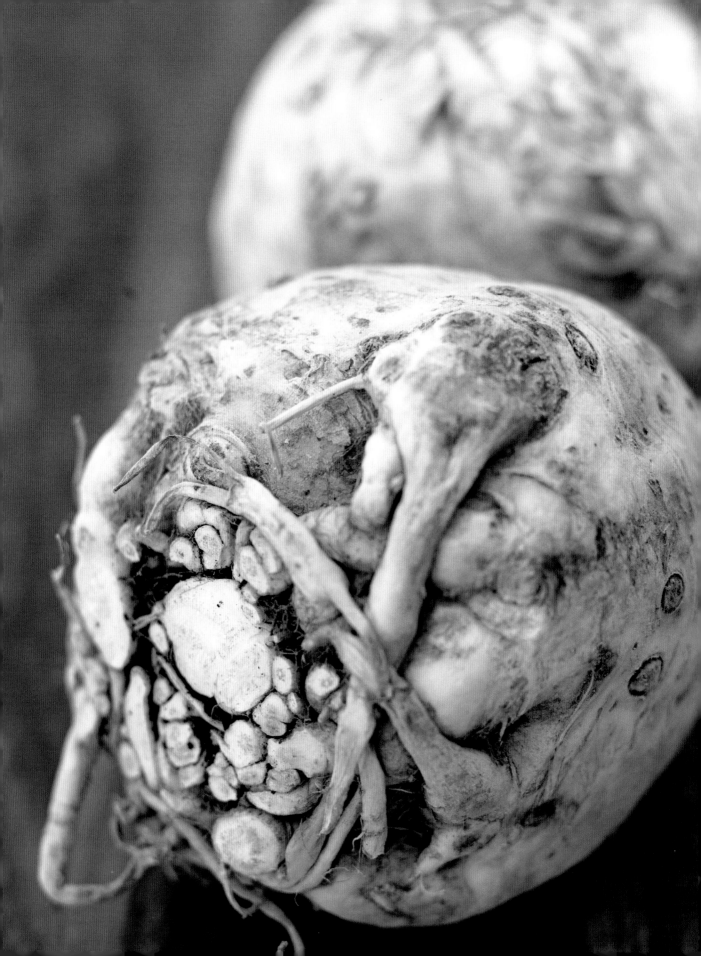

celeriac

Man, the celeriac is one ugly vegetable. It's a shame really. It looks so ferocious, but its flavour is gentle; it just gives off a hint of celery and tastes almost nutty. It's soft, like a firm, mild celery, but not crunchy. It makes a fine soup – in fact it does everything a potato can do and more, as it can be eaten raw in salads if grated. We don't use celeriac much over here and that's a real shame. The French love it; in restaurants and bistros all over the country you'll find celeriac *rémoulade* – firm strips of celeriac with a mustardy gherkin-flavoured mayonnaise. Yummy!

Many people suggest mixing celeriac with mashed potato to make celeriac mash, but I think that just disguises the celeriac flavour and messes about with simple mashed potato.

Getting the skin off celeriac can be troublesome. My advice is to cut it into thin slices and then chop away the skin around the circumference of the circle shape you are left with. Have a bowl of acidulated water nearby to drop the slices into as the flesh will discolour when exposed to the air.

Celeriac is a close relative of celery. Celeriac is not actually a root vegetable; it is an underground swollen stem that grows above the roots. One last thing, celery salt comes from celeriac, not celery.

a few facts about celeriac

There is no mention of celeriac in Britain until its seeds appeared in an 18th century seed catalogue, where it was described as an Arabic vegetable. It was known as a delicacy in some parts of the world before this, but then it was the stem of a wild plant known as 'smallage' (also the ancestor of celery).

buying celeriac

Try to find celeriac with as smooth a skin as possible so you don't waste any flesh when peeling it. It should feel heavy and there should be no cracks in the skin. The top is the part that starts to soften first, so look at this and press it with your finger, then turn it over and give it a good prodding as the underbelly softens next.

storing celeriac

You don't have to use celeriac all in one go. Cut some off, wrap it in clingfilm and put it back in the fridge. Uncut it will last for up to 2 weeks; cut it will last for 3–4 days.

preparing raw celeriac

Peel the celeriac and keep it in acidulated water until you want to use it. Slice very thinly on a mandolin, grate or cut into julienne strips and serve with dips.
Try: in a salad – either grated or finely sliced.

jan	feb	mar	apr	may	jun	jul	aug	sep	oct	nov	dec

puréeing celeriac

This is a brilliant rich, creamy purée. Peel the celeriac and cut it into 2cm (¾ inch) cubes. Keep these cubes in acidulated water as you go. Bring a pan of just enough salted water to the boil. Add the celeriac, reduce the heat and simmer, lid on, for about 15–20 minutes, until soft – they will break up during cooking if boiled too fast. Drain well. Whiz in a food processor, adding butter and single cream until you get the texture you want. Taste and season before serving.

Try with: pork chops.

roasting celeriac

Preheat the oven to 190°C/375°F/gas mark 5. Put a roasting tin with 1cm (½ inch) of vegetable oil into the oven to heat. Peel the celeriac and cut it into chunks the size you can handle. Keep these chunks in acidulated water as you go. Bring a pan of just enough salted water to the boil. Add the celeriac, reduce the heat and simmer, lid on, for 4 minutes. Drain well. Remove the tin from the oven and coat the celeriac in the oil. Season well, then roast in the top of the oven until the celeriac is brown, soft and tender, about 40 minutes. Remember to turn occasionally. Alternatively, you can roast them beside your joint.

Try with: any roast meats.

celeriac crisps with aïoli

As nibbles go, these are very fine. The only word of warning is that they are moreish.
I fear you may have a few too many, so if you're drinking, make sure someone stays sober
in case you want to fry some more. I am giving no quantities here, as this is a snack.
I don't know how many crisps you eat, or how much dip you like on the end of each nibble.

aïoli (see page 101)
chives, chopped, to taste
celeriac
sunflower oil
rock salt, to serve

Mix the aïoli with the chopped chives. Keep in the fridge until you're ready to eat it.

Cut the ends off the celeriac and peel it. Thinly slice it on a mandolin and keep in acidulated water as you go.

Put the slices on kitchen towel to soak up excess moisture.

Heat the oil in a heavy-based pan; it is ready when a cube of bread dropped into it sizzles. Be careful!

Fry the celeriac slices for a couple of minutes or so, until golden brown. Do not put all the slices in at once, as the oil temperature will drop and the crisps will get greasy.

Dry the crisps on kitchen towel. Serve with plenty of rock salt and the aïoli for dipping.

celeriac beef rolls

When you prepare this you'll probably worry that there is too much mustard and horseradish. Don't worry – this dish cooks for a long time, so while the flavour of the mustard and horseradish remains, the fire is cooked out. This dish makes winter worthwhile. Cook it, put on an old black and white film, and munch on the sofa.

serves 4

700g (1lb 9oz) silverside of beef, sliced into 8 slices

1 onion, finely sliced

3 carrots, grated

175g (6oz) celeriac, peeled, grated and sprinkled with lemon juice

3 tbsp Dijon mustard

2 tbsp creamed horseradish

salt and black pepper

25g (1oz) butter

2 tbsp vegetable oil

2 tbsp plain flour

300ml (10fl oz) beef stock

4 tbsp sherry

5 tbsp chopped parsley

Preheat the oven to 180°C/350°F/gas mark 4.

Place each slice of meat between 2 pieces of clingfilm, then bash it with a rolling pin until thin and even.

Place the onion, carrots and celeriac in a pan, cover with cold salted water, and bring to the boil. Drain as soon as it comes to the boil.

Stir half the mustard and half the horseradish into the cooked vegetables and season.

Remove the clingfilm from the beef. Put an 8th of the vegetable mixture on to each slice. Roll the beef around the mixture into a sausage shape, tucking in the sides of the beef where you can. Secure each roll with a wooden cocktail stick.

Heat the butter and oil together in a pan. Add the beef rolls and cook over a medium heat, turning them regularly, until brown all over. Transfer to a casserole dish.

Return the pan to the heat. Add the flour, and stir. Gradually pour in the stock, and whisk. Add the sherry, the rest of the mustard and horseradish, and the parsley. Bring to the boil, then remove from the heat immediately.

Pour the sauce over the beef rolls. Cover the casserole dish with a lid or kitchen foil and bake for 1½ hours. Remove the cocktail sticks before serving.

braised celeriac in cider with sausages and apple

I love winter. My brother Biffo knows this and claims I can be no brother of his. But I think I like it grey and rainy so I can enjoy dishes like this.

serves 4

3 tbsp vegetable oil

450g (1lb) good sausages

2 onions, finely sliced

1 tbsp plain flour

400ml (14fl oz) dry cider

350g (12oz) celeriac, peeled, cut into large dice and sprinkled with lemon juice

1 tbsp Worcestershire sauce

1 tbsp roughly chopped sage

salt and black pepper

1 medium cooking apple, peeled, cored and sliced

Preheat the oven to 180°C/350°F/gas mark 4.

Heat the oil in a frying pan over a medium heat. Fry the sausages quickly until brown all over. Transfer to a casserole dish.

Return the frying pan to the heat, add the onions and fry for a few minutes, until they are dark golden. Stir in the flour, then gradually pour in the cider. Bring to the boil, stirring all the time. Add the celeriac and cook for 2 minutes. Stir in the Worcestershire sauce and sage. Season.

Pour this over the sausages, cover with a lid or kitchen foil and bake for 30 minutes. Scatter over the apple slices and cook, covered, for a further 15 minutes.

celery

Celery is a pretty plant. Too many of us see weak-coloured celery cropped off at the top, and therefore missing its foliage. And what is it doing in those plastic bags? When I first started working with Secretts Farm in Surrey, the pace of the place disturbed me. I couldn't understand why nothing happened as quickly as I wanted it to. After one season of working on the farm, I realised why. Farms aren't supposed to work quickly; Mother Nature controls the pace. But it's well worth the wait, and a field of large green celery, with all those leaves intact, is one of the most stunning sights you'll see on a farm.

I am always surprised at the strong reaction celery can bring out in people. Many like it, a good few are indifferent, but those who dislike it really dislike it. I've always thought, even as a child, that at its best celery smells slightly of pineapple. We often eat it raw, I mean it's great raw – like the spring onion, it becomes a natural dipper, a big, long-handled one. With a bit of salt, it's a perfect accompaniment for cheese – the crunch of a fibrous, juicy celery stalk acts as a perfect cleanser to a mouthful of sticky Gloucester or Stilton, but at the same time it remains a very savoury food.

But I love celery cooked, too. It braises fantastically; those fibres soften down and the texture is superb. It also acts like a sponge for any stronger flavours it's braised in, while still holding its own. This is a great quality in a vegetable. The great culinary nations of Europe realised celery's potential for cooking years ago. It's a major player in the French *mirepoix*, the Italian *sofrito* and the Spanish *sofregit*. All these are different names for the same chopped vegetables that form the base of so many dishes.

I urge you to buy celery with the leaves intact. The leaves are perfect for adding flavour to stocks or stews. I feel I should confess that for years, when chefs ordered lovage, we would often send them leaves from the celery stalk, and no one ever complained. Celery leaves do a perfect impersonation of lovage!

Celery salt is made from celeriac, not celery. What can be used as a seasoning from the celery plant are the seeds. Celeriac is the swollen stem of a celery, but it is a different variety from the stuff we eat. Celery that you buy in the shops will not have a bulbous celeriac root, just as a celeriac will not have a bright green vibrant celery on the end of it. They are closely related cousins, but they are not the same.

A few callers to my Radio 4 show *Veg Talk* are searching for white sooty celery. I've tried it, and a very fine product it is too. For those who don't know, it's a normal celery plant, but it's been 'blanched'. In growing terms, this means keeping it away from light. And guess what was piled around sooty celery to keep it from light? Soot, of course! Nobody seems to produce it on a scale bigger than for domestic use.

a few facts about celery

Celery was considered by the Romans to be an aphrodisiac. Wild celery was gathered by the Greeks. It is mentioned in Homer's *Odyssey* and was used as a garland for Olympic Games winners. In Britain, the herb was gathered from the wild before it

jan	feb	mar	apr	may	jun	jul	aug	sep	oct	nov	dec

was farmed. The wild herb was called smallage and was used as a laxative or dried or crushed and put into small bags that were held to the noses of people of quality when they went somewhere smelly. The first mention of celery as a veg is in 15th century Italy. From there, it spread across the rest of Europe by the height of the Renaissance.

buying celery
Try to buy celery with the leaves intact; this is the best indication of freshness. The leaves are the first things on the plant to deteriorate.

storing celery
Store celery upright in the fridge in cold water, where it will last for up to 4 days. The celery will suck up lots, I mean an amazing amount, of cold water, so that when you bite into it, it will explode with juice and flavour. Before cooking, wash, wash and wash again. Celery and the earth become the closest of friends, and parting them is never easy.

preparing raw celery
Pull any leaves off the celery and cut away the base and any brown or dry edges. Peel it lightly with a vegetable peeler. Slice into bite-size chunks.
Try with: strong cheese.

braising celery
Preheat the oven to 180°C/350°F/gas mark 4. Pull any leaves off the celery and cut away the base and any brown or dry edges. Put the celery in an ovenproof dish, add a crushed clove of garlic and 1 tbsp of white wine vinegar for every celery head, and cover with chicken stock. Cover with kitchen foil and cook for 40 minutes. Drain off any liquid.
Try with: melted cheese.

steaming celery
Pull any leaves off the celery and cut away the base and any brown or dry edges. Remove the stalks and cut them in half across the middle and again lengthways so they fit the sieve. Bring a pan of salted water to the boil and, when plenty of steam has built up, sit the sieve over the pan (it mustn't touch the water). Cook, lid on, for 5 minutes.
Try with: fish.

braised celery hearts

Braising celery gives it a deeper but smoother flavour – and this braising liquid is good enough to drink. Still, you wouldn't want to eat braised celery on its own; a mouthful maybe, but not a plateful. Melting blue cheese on it will make sure the bowl is emptied!

serves 4

4 celery hearts
50g (1³/₄oz) butter
2 cloves of garlic, crushed
200ml (7fl oz) chicken stock
2 tbsp white wine vinegar
100g (3¹/₂oz) Stilton cheese

Preheat the oven to 180°C/350°F/gas mark 4.

Pull any leaves off the celery and cut away the base and any brown or dry edges.

Melt the butter in a pan over a medium heat and cook the hearts, turning occasionally, until they colour, about 5 minutes.

Remove the pan from the heat and drain off the excess butter. Put the celery in an ovenproof dish along with the garlic, stock and vinegar. Cover the dish with foil and bake for 40 minutes.

Remove from the oven and drain off the excess liquid (actually, drink it; it's magnificent). Crumble over the cheese and return to the oven for 5 minutes, until the cheese melts.

London Particular soup

This is a very old-fashioned recipe. I have no idea where it comes from, but dishes like this should survive.

serves 6

25g (1oz) butter
6 rashers streaky bacon, diced
1 onion, chopped
3 stalks of celery, finely sliced
2 carrots, roughly chopped
450g (1lb) dried peas, soaked overnight
2.3 litres (4 pints) vegetable or chicken stock
bouquet garni
1 tbsp Worcestershire sauce
salt and black pepper

Melt the butter in a large pan over a medium heat and add the bacon. Cook for about 5 minutes, then add the chopped onion, sliced celery and chopped carrots, cover with a lid, and sweat for 10 minutes.

Meanwhile, drain the soaked peas and add them to the pot with the stock and bouquet garni. Bring to the boil and simmer, lid on, for 45 minutes.

Whiz with a hand-held blender. Season with Worcestershire sauce and salt and pepper.

chard

Like a master of disguise, this veg has many names: chard, Swiss chard, spinach beet and blette. It is a truly great vegetable; I list it among my all-time favourites. It has a long stem with leaves attached on both sides near the top. It has the most delicious of crunches and releases much flavoursome juice, and its leaves taste of spinach, though much softer. Both leaves and stem are very tender. What's more, it needs hardly any cooking; I cook the stem and leaves together, but you can separate them.

types of chard

Chard comes in an array of colours: green, white, yellow, red and sometimes combinations of all 4. The chard I knew when I worked in Covent Garden was a big ugly vegetable, sometimes more than a foot wide, split at the ends, with huge coarse umbrella-like leaves sprouting out from its ugly stalk, and tied up with string in case it tried to escape. I could see no reason for its existence. It wasn't until I started working at Secretts Farm and saw the chard harvested as it should be, with a stem no thicker than my thumb, that I began to appreciate it.

Chard is actually a type of beet. If you are lucky enough to see beetroot growing, you will see that the stems and leaves are nearly identical to chard. I have no idea why it isn't more popular, although it may be because it deteriorates quickly. It is more popular in the Mediterranean, but even then not huge.

a few facts about chard

Chard is more popular in the Arab world than it is in the West. It's said to have grown in the fabled gardens of Babylon. I have no idea why it's called 'Swiss', but by the 19th century this word was being added to the name in seed catalogues.

buying chard

Look for thin stems no thicker than your thumb, and soft leaves.

storing chard

Unfortunately, even if you've bought it just after harvesting, the chard will last no longer than 3 days in your refrigerator.

boiling chard leaves and stems

Chop the leaves and stems into 10cm (4 inch) pieces, keeping them separate. Cut away any very stringy bits. Bring a large pan of salted water to the boil. Wash the veg. Add the chopped stems to the pan; cook for 1 minutes before adding the chopped leaves. Cook for a further 2–3 minutes, until soft. Drain.
Try with: butter and a scrape of nutmeg.

| jan | feb | mar | apr | may | jun | jul | aug | sep | oct | nov | dec |

cooking chard leaves and stems in cream

This is my favourite way to cook this veg. Follow the instructions for boiling chard leaves and stems. Mix with 40ml (1½fl oz) of single cream, 5g (⅛oz) of butter and 1 tsp of chopped chervil for every 100g (3½oz) of chard.

Try with: sticky, soft chicken.

pan-finishing chard leaves and stems

Follow the instructions for boiling chard leaves and stems. Melt 1–2 tsp of butter per 100g (3½oz) of chard in a pan, add the chard and a couple of gratings of nutmeg and cook until warmed through.

Try with: veal or pork.

steaming chard leaves and stems

Chop the leaves and stems into 10cm (4 inch) pieces. Cut away any very stringy bits. Wash the chopped pieces well and put them in a sieve. Bring a pan of salted water to the boil and wait for a good amount of steam to build up before adding the chard. Sit the sieve over the pan of boiling water – ensure it does not touch the water – and cover with the lid. Cook for 7 minutes, until soft.

Try with: fish.

steaming chard leaves

Rip the leaves from the stem. Put them in a pan with the water still clinging to them from washing. Cook for up to 4–7 minutes, depending on the thickness of the leaves, stirring regularly, until soft.

Try with: any meat or fish.

chard frittata

My advice when you're making up recipes is: if it tastes right to you then other people will like it. I obviously don't trust my own advice because when I made this up I handed it to neighbours to try before I included it in the book. They loved it.

serves 4
25g (1oz) butter
3 tbsp sunflower oil
1 small onion, cut into
5mm (¹/₄ inch) dice
200g (7oz) chard
salt and black pepper
5 eggs
5 tbsp freshly grated Parmesan

Melt the butter with the oil in a frying pan over a low heat. Add the onion and cook for 10 minutes, until soft but not brown.

Trim off any rough bits at the bottom of the chard and wash well. Chop the chard and add it, along with some salt and pepper, to the onion. Cook, stirring occasionally, until the chard is soft – about 5 minutes.

Meanwhile, crack the eggs into a clean bowl. Add the Parmesan and beat well. Pour the mixture over the chard, still on the heat, and stir. Leave it alone now; the bottom will cook first.

When the whole thing moves as one but the top is still a wet raw mix, place under a medium grill for 5–10 minutes, until the top firms. Serve cold.

chard gratin

Boy, this is good. The flavours are obvious. You can see, looking at the ingredients, that this is going to be packed with flavour. But it is the texture that delights me: the slight crunch of the chard, the dry stickiness that comes with goat's cheese, and the juice of good tomatoes.

serves 4

1kg (2lb 4oz) chard
salt and black pepper
2 tbsp white wine vinegar
5 tbsp olive oil
4 cloves of garlic, finely chopped
500g (1lb 2oz) tomatoes, peeled and sliced
100g (3¹/₂oz) soft goat's cheese
75g (2³/₄oz) French bread, with crusts on, whizzed to breadcrumbs
2 tsp thyme leaves

Preheat the oven to 180°C/350°F/gas mark 4.

Trim off any rough bits at the bottom of the chard. Remove the leaves from the stalks and cut the stalks in half. Wash well.

Bring a large pan of salted water to the boil and add the vinegar.

Cook the stalks in the pan of boiling water for 3 minutes. Fish them out and drain well; they retain plenty of liquid.

Drop the leaves into the boiling water and cook for 2 minutes. Drain and squeeze out as much water as you can.

Heat 2 tbsp of the olive oil in a wok over a medium heat. Add half the garlic. When sizzling, add the cooked chard stalks. Season and gently fry for 2 minutes. Remove the stalks from the pan.

Add the rest of the garlic and 2 tbsp of the olive oil to the wok. When the garlic is sizzling, add the chard leaves and cook for 2 minutes. Remove the wok from the heat and remove the leaves.

Put half the stalks and leaves in the bottom of a gratin dish. Cover with half the tomatoes and season. Top with half the cheese. Repeat the process.

Mix the breadcrumbs in a bowl with the thyme and the rest of the oil. Sprinkle this on top of the gratin. Bake for 30 minutes.

chard pasties

I ate these warm when I made them, then I had another one cold for breakfast. I preferred them warm, but my mate Zed liked them cold. Before trying this, I would never have believed I could enjoy a pasty with so little meat.

serves 4

for the shortcrust pastry
300g (10½oz) plain flour
150g (5½oz) cold butter, plus extra for greasing
1 egg, beaten, for glazing

for the filling
700g (1lb 9oz) chard
60g (2¼oz) butter
1 onion, chopped
80g (2¾oz) streaky bacon, chopped
50g (1¾oz) Cheddar, grated
25g (1oz) fresh breadcrumbs
15g (½oz) sage, chopped
6 tbsp crème fraîche
salt and black pepper

To make the pastry, sieve the flour into a bowl. Cut the butter (it should be as cold as possible) into small chunks and rub into the flour using your fingertips, until the mixture looks like coarse breadcrumbs. Carefully add 1–2 tbsp of cold water, and bring it together with your hands – you want a soft but rollable dough. Wrap in clingfilm and refrigerate for an hour.

Preheat the oven to 200°C/400°F/gas mark 6 and grease a baking sheet with butter.

Trim the very bottom, tough bit of the chard stalk and wash well. Chop the leaves and the stem together into very small pieces.

Put the chard in a pan with half the butter. Cover and cook over a low heat for 8 minutes. Strain the chard well as it will be full of moisture. Put the drained chard in a large bowl.

Melt the rest of the butter in a frying pan over a medium heat. Add the onion and bacon and fry until the onion is soft and the bacon has browned. Tip them into the bowl with the chard.

Stir in the cheese, breadcrumbs, sage and crème fraîche, and season well.

Roll out the pastry and, using a side plate as a mould, cut out 4 rounds. Spoon the filling equally into the middle of the rounds.

Brush water over the edges of the rounds and bring the edges together. Press along the join with your finger and thumb to make a pretty pattern. Make sure the pasty is completely sealed. Brush with beaten egg.

Bake on a greased baking sheet for about 20 minutes, until the pastry is golden.

ribollita

This is an Italian dish, and its name means 're-boiled'. There are lots and lots of veg in here, all cooking very slowly, with all those flavours melting into each other. Perfect for summer, spring, autumn or winter.

serves 4

4 tbsp olive oil

1 red onion, finely chopped

15g (¹/₂oz) parsley, finely chopped

2 cloves of garlic, finely chopped

225g (8oz) chard (or leaf spinach), roughly chopped

1 loose green cabbage, roughly chopped

2 celery stalks

1 bulb of fennel, thinly sliced

2 litres (3¹/₂ pints) vegetable or chicken stock

1 bouquet garni

2 courgettes (green or yellow), thinly sliced

2 tbsp pesto

400g tin borlotti, haricot or pinto beans

400g tin chopped tomatoes

salt and black pepper

Parmesan, freshly grated, to serve

extra virgin olive oil, to serve

Heat the olive oil in a large pan over a medium heat. Add the onion, parsley and garlic and cook to soften for 5 minutes.

Set aside half the chard or spinach, cabbage and celery. Add the other half to the onion mixture with all the fennel. Sweat, lid on, for 10 minutes. Add the stock and bouquet garni, and simmer, lid off, for 1 hour.

Add the courgettes, pesto, beans and tomatoes to the pan and simmer, lid off, for 20 minutes.

Towards the end of the cooking time, bring a large pan of salted water to the boil. Drop in the reserved chard or spinach, cabbage and celery, and boil for 2 minutes.

Add the blanched greens to the soup, season, and serve drizzled with extra virgin olive oil and grated Parmesan.

chicory

Most of us see chicory as a salad leaf and, I have to confess, this is mostly how I use it. Those crisp whitish-yellow leaves are crunchy and so charmingly bitter. They are also very handy, as that spearhead shape that curls upwards and inwards around the edges makes them the perfect holding vessels for other foods, rather like little salad plates. They are a vegetable though, and when softly braised they lose that bitterness while retaining their crunch in most of the leaf.

types of chicory

What we Brits know as 'chicory' the French call 'endive' (we call curly lettuce 'endive') and the Belgians call 'witloof'. **Red chicory**, which is a very pleasing deep red with white veins, tastes exactly the same as the **white** stuff. In fact radicchio, that now obligatory salad item, is a type of chicory. Belgian growers developed white chicory by blanching it – that is, piling up earth around it as it grew to make sure no sun got to it.

a few facts about chicory

Chicory was developed from a wild plant found in West Asia and Africa. It was known to the Greeks and Romans in its wild form. Cultivated chicory appeared relatively recently. Allegedly a Belgian gardener grew it by accident and gave it to his wife, who loved it. When he died, a friend of his grew it and shared it with the wife and others.

buying and storing chicory

Check the edges of the chicory for any sign of browning. Once they go, boy do they go; one minute you got a crisp yellow salad head, the next you have a bar of melting chocolate. The head should be tight and the leaves close in on one another. If they start to curl outwards they're going. Chicory will last in the fridge for up to a week.

braising chicory

Preheat the oven to 180°C/350°F/gas mark 4. Wash and trim 4 heads of chicory. Melt 25g (1oz) butter in a frying pan over a low heat. Add the chicory and cook for 5 minutes. Transfer to a baking dish and add 250ml (9fl oz) vegetable stock. Bake for 15 minutes.
Try with: duck.

cooking chicory in butter or cream

Wash the chicory and trim off the base. Bring a pan of salted water to the boil, add the chicory and boil, lid off, for 10–12 minutes. Drain, squeezing the veg. Return it to the pan with a knob of butter and 2 tbsp of vegetable stock per head. Cook, lid off, on a high heat for 3–4 minutes, until the liquid has evaporated. For creamed chicory, once the stock has almost evaporated add a little single cream and grate in a little nutmeg.
Try with: ham.

jan	feb	mar	apr	may	jun	jul	aug	sep	oct	nov	dec

chicory and crab salad

Chicory, like me, needs a partner. On its own, it is dull and a bit bitter. With this dish, not only does the bitter flavour enhance the natural sweetness of the crab, but it also acts as a wonderful base for the delightful mixture.

serves 4

450g (1lb) cooked white and/or brown crabmeat

1 tbsp olive oil

2 tbsp chopped parsley

2 red chillies, de-seeded and finely chopped

1 tsp freshly grated ginger

juice of 3 limes

salt and black pepper

2 heads of chicory

Mix all the ingredients apart from the chicory in a bowl with your fingers. This is your recipe – you are going to eat it, so increase or decrease the amount of each ingredient as it suits you.

Discard the outer leaves of the chicory heads and cut away the brown bottoms. Pull off as many leaves as you want and lay them on a plate.

Spoon the crab mixture on to the chicory and eat with your fingers.

chicory with mustard cream

This recipe takes the sharp edge off the chicory without removing its unique flavour, and I love it.

serves 4

25g (1oz) butter

1 onion, finely sliced

4 heads of chicory

250ml (9fl oz) vegetable or chicken stock

juice of 1 lemon

120ml (4fl oz) single cream

2 tsp Dijon mustard

salt and black pepper

25g (1oz) cooked ham, finely sliced

2 tbsp chopped parsley

Melt the butter in a frying pan over a medium heat. Add the onion and cook for 5 minutes, until softened.

Discard the outer leaves of the chicory heads and cut away the brown bottoms.

Reduce the heat to low, then add the chicory, cover, and cook for a further 5 minutes.

Pour in the stock and lemon juice, increase the heat to medium, and simmer, covered, for 15 minutes, until the chicory is cooked.

Remove the chicory from the pan and place in a serving bowl. Keep warm. Boil the remaining liquid in the pan until reduced to approximately 120ml (4fl oz). Pour in the cream and mustard and simmer for 5 minutes.

Season and stir in the ham and parsley. Serve the chicory with the sauce poured over the top.

chillies

There are two daddies of the chilli world: the Thai birdseye and the Mexican habañero. I've been to Mexico, where the chilli originated, and there I've seen old guys sitting around a table munching whole raw habañeros as a starter. This I don't understand. I am a blue-collar boy, brought up in a rough area of South-East London. Like many others, I convinced myself that there were things I had to do to become a man. But one ritual that I never felt duty-bound to join in with was hunting down and eating the hottest dish I could find on a Saturday night.

Chillies are virtually universal. One of my favourites is the padrón in Spain, which is unique in that it is usually mild, but around 1 in 25 is red hot. The Spanish fry them whole in a little oil and much salt and serve them like that. Waiting for the hot one is like a culinary form of Russian roulette. They also love chillies in southern Italy, particularly in the mountainous regions of Calabria, where chillies can be seen hanging and drying in bunches on doors and window ledges. Chillies, originally from Central America, are big players in the cuisines of South America, North and West Africa, India, South-East Asia and the southern states of the US. India is the biggest producer.

When cooking chillies, remember that you can add but you can't take away. Taste as you go, adding heat if you want to. There is more heat in the seed and white pith than there is in the flesh, so I always add the flesh to a dish, then if I want more heat I add the pith and step up to the seed if it still needs it. If you burn your mouth eating chillies, water or beer won't help; go for a dairy product such as yoghurt or a starchy food such as rice. As well as heat, if used subtly, chillies can give an almost fruity flavour. The mild heat of chilli can act as either an irritant or stimulant and enhance appetite.

types of chillies

Chillies are capsicums, which means they are a type of pepper. There are literally hundreds of varieties; there are over 150 in Mexico alone. This makes classification almost impossible. These are the varieties most commonly found in Britain:

Anaheim: Very long, thin and pointed. They are sold green and red and this is what you see most commonly in the shops. They range from mild to hot.

Birdseye: This is a tiny specimen; most are half the size of your little finger and as thin as the tube inside a biro. They are even hotter than the habañero.

Habañero: Sometimes known as the **Scotch bonnet**, other times known as the **lantern**. It looks like a squashed cube or a Chinese lantern. Be careful, it is seriously hot.

Jalapeño: This is the chilli you get on your American Hot pizza. It is almost oval. I think of it as half-hot: spicy certainly, but bearable.

Poblano: These are pointy, green and as big, if not bigger, than the bell peppers you find in every supermarket. They have much more flavour than a pepper but are very mild. This is the perfect chilli for stuffing. When red, they are called **ancho**.

jan	feb	mar	apr	may	jun	jul	aug	sep	oct	nov	dec

Serrano: A small, rounded chilli, mainly eaten while still green, which gives about as much heat as a jalapeño.

a few facts about chillies

Chillies originated in Central America in the area we now know as Mexico. They were gathered there wild from an amazing 7,000BC, and farmed from 3,500BC. Spanish and Portuguese explorers and traders took them to India and South-East Asia, from where they spread through the Middle East, into the Balkans, and on into Europe.

buying and storing chillies

As a rule of thumb, usually the smaller chillies are the hotter they are. Check the skin before you buy to make sure it's not wrinkled and there are no wet spots. I don't refrigerate chillies; I think the cold impairs the flavour. Unrefrigerated they can last for 3 or 4 days; double that if you do put them in the fridge.

chicken wings with salsa

I have given the recipe for the chicken wings and the salsa separately.

serves 4

for the salsa

1 green chilli
4 tomatoes, peeled and chopped
2 cloves of garlic, crushed
2 spring onions, finely sliced
1 tbsp sherry vinegar
1 tbsp tomato ketchup

for the chicken wings

1 tbsp vegetable oil
1 shallot, finely chopped
2 cloves of garlic, crushed
2 tbsp clear honey
4 tbsp tomato ketchup
4 tbsp Worcestershire sauce
2 tbsp English mustard
2 tbsp hot pepper sauce
16 chicken wings, tips cut off

For the salsa, deseed and finely chop the chilli. Mix together all the ingredients in a bowl and season to taste. Set aside for at least 1 hour.

Preheat the oven to 220°C/425°F/gas mark 7.

For the chicken wings, heat the oil in a small pan over a medium heat and add the shallot and garlic. Fry gently for 2–3 minutes, until soft. Add all the other ingredients apart from the wings and simmer gently for 2 minutes. Coat the wings in the sauce.

Put the wings and sauce in a roasting tin. Place in the oven for about 30 minutes, until brown and sticky and the chicken is cooked through.

Serve the wings with the tomato salsa.

stuffed chillies

This dish can be mild or as hot as a space rocket – depending, of course, on what chilli you decide to use. I would pick something mild, as the stuffing is packed with flavour. If you want your guests to get drunk, use hotter chillies so they drink more!

serves 4

10 large poblano chillies

5 sausages

1 egg, beaten

25g (1oz) breadcrumbs

2 cloves of garlic, finely chopped

1 shallot, finely chopped

3 mild peppadew peppers (from a jar), drained and finely chopped

2 tbsp chopped fresh parsley

salt and black pepper

olive oil

Preheat the oven to 200°C/400°F/gas mark 6 and grease a roasting tin.

Halve the chillies. Deseed them, but keep the stalks on. Take the sausagemeat out of the skins.

Combine the sausagemeat with all the other ingredients, except for the chillies and olive oil.

Stuff the chilli halves with the meat mixture – the stuffing should take up as much room as the missing half chilli.

Put the stuffed chillies in the roasting tin. Drizzle with olive oil and roast for 15–20 minutes, until brown.

chilli con carne

I've loved this chilli since I was a kid.

serves 4

500g (1lb 2oz) minced beef

1 tbsp olive oil

1 large onion, finely chopped

1 tsp ground cumin

1 tsp ground coriander

2 tsp chilli powder

2 tbsp tomato purée

4 red Anaheim chillies, deseeded (or not) and chopped

400g tin chopped tomatoes

410g tin kidney beans, drained

salt and black pepper

1 tsp caster sugar

10g (¼oz) dark chocolate

Heat a frying pan over a high heat. Add the mince and fry until brown; don't poke it. Remove from the pan and set the meat aside in a bowl.

Reduce the heat to medium. Using the same pan, heat the olive oil, then add the onion and fry until softened and lightly browned, about 10 minutes.

Return the mince to the pan. Add the spices, tomato purée and chopped chilli and cook, stirring, for 2 minutes.

Add the tomatoes, beans, salt and pepper to taste, and the sugar. Simmer for about an hour, lid on, until the liquid has thickened.

Crumble in the chocolate and simmer for 5 minutes, until melted.

chilli and garlic oil

In Calabria in southern Italy, people have chillies hanging, drying, on their front doors. They call them *diavolino*, meaning 'little devil'. They use chilli oil like people in the rest of Italy use Parmesan. A bottle of this oil will stay good in your cupboard for ages.

makes 500ml (18fl oz)
3 birdseye chillies
5 large dried red chillies
2 tsp black peppercorns
500ml (18fl oz) extra-virgin olive oil
6 cloves of garlic, finely chopped

Halve the birdseye chillies and finely chop 3 of the dried red chillies. Roughly crush half the peppercorns.

Heat 4 tbsp of the olive oil in a frying pan over a low heat. Add the birdseye chillies, the finely chopped dried chillies and the garlic, and cook for 2 minutes to release their flavour.

Pour the remaining oil into a large sterilized storage jar and add the fried chilli mixture and the crushed and whole peppercorns. Seal tightly and store for 2–3 weeks.

Strain the oil to remove all the bits, then transfer to a sterilized bottle (or bottles), adding a couple of dried chillies. Seal and store in a dark place.

chilli and garlic oil with prawns

Peeling prawns is a bit messy but, that aside, this dish takes minutes to prepare and cook. I use 3 chillies, but you should use as many or as few as you want.

serves 4
225g (8oz) raw prawns
3 tbsp olive oil
2 cloves of garlic, finely sliced
3 red Anaheim chillies, deseeded and finely chopped

Pull the heads from the prawns and peel each prawn by opening the shell along the body and peeling it away from the flesh. For larger prawns, remove the dark string down the back. Leave the tails intact.

Heat the oil in a wok over a medium to high heat. When it is hot but not smoking (olive oil burns easily), add the garlic and chilli and cook, stirring, for 1 minute – this will flavour the oil.

Add the prawns. Cook, stirring, until the prawns are pink – about 2 minutes. Serve straightaway.

chilli jam with squid

Oh, it's a tricky beast, the squid. It needs to be either cooked quickly or slowly. Anything in between and it's big chew time! The best squid and jam I've tasted was at Smiths of Smithfield, run by my co-judge on MasterChef Goes Large, John Torode.

serves 4

for the jam

2 birdseye chillies, chopped, seeds left in

125g (4¹/₂oz) granulated sugar

2 cloves of garlic, crushed

1 tsp chopped fresh ginger

50ml (2fl oz) red wine vinegar

230g tin chopped tomatoes

for the squid

500g (1lb 2oz) squid

seasoned flour

1 litre (1³/₄ pints) sunflower oil

For the jam, put all the ingredients in a pan and cook on a low heat for 1 hour, lid off, stirring occasionally. Remove from the heat and allow to cool.

To prepare the squid, pull the head and intestines from the body. Cut the tentacles from the head and set aside, then squeeze out the beak-like mouth. Pull the plastic-like quill from the body, then pull off the fins. Remove the semi-transparent skin, wash out the pouch and dry thoroughly on kitchen towel.

Cut the squid into rings as wide as your index finger. Leave the tentacle bits as they are. Toss the rings and tentacles in the seasoned flour.

Heat the oil in a frying pan. The oil is ready when it bubbles furiously around anything dropped in it such as a cube of bread – be careful!

Drop in the squid. Stir for 30 seconds as soon as you drop the squid in – this is to stop it sticking to pan. Cook for 2 minutes.

Carefully remove the squid from the oil and place on kitchen towel to drain. Put the jam in ramekins and serve with the squid.

courgettes and marrows

The first time I tried a courgette that had been sliced lengthways and griddled with a little olive oil was a revelation. Cutting through the firm, yellow, green-edged flesh with those brown caramelized stripes that only a griddle can give was a real pleasure, and led to my first experience of the subtle tang of this vegetable. Before that I'd only tried courgettes that had been boiled in a great big pan of water for what I'd guess was about 3½ weeks! The result was slush. Courgettes are over 90 per cent water, so anything other than very quick cooking will ruin them.

The courgette is a cucurbit, which means that it comes from the same family as the cucumber, the squash and the melon. It is actually a small, young summer squash. Courgettes appeared in Britain very late compared with the rest of the world, probably at least in part through the efforts of the food writer Elizabeth David, but they have been enjoyed in Europe's Mediterranean countries for a long time.

courgette flowers

I adore courgette flowers. They are real, natural and delicate, with big, bright, yellow flowers. These flowers should be enjoyed for themselves, not messed about with or stuffed with strong flavours such as crab. I've even seen them stuffed with mince. There are exceptions; I've tasted a good courgette flower risotto at the River Café. But the only way I really like to eat these flowers is dipped in a light batter and shallow-fried.

I've devoted half a greenhouse with raised beds to these beauties. They are so expensive because they are hard to harvest. The flowers only open with the first of the morning sunshine, and if you don't harvest them within a few hours they close in on themselves. So in summer, at sun-up, my partner Vernon and I arm ourselves with scissors and trays and wade, shoulder-deep, through courgette plants, snipping off each flower.

There are Dutch courgette flowers that seem incapable of rotting. I'm not a scientist, but I do know that veg rots quickly. I find non-rotting veg scary. These Dutch flowers come in triangular plastic packets; avoid them like the plague. Normal courgette flowers have to be bought and eaten that day; any longer and they close in.

marrows

The marrow is a big fat courgette. I like it. It is much better value than the courgette, although it's not big on flavour. It's great stuffed. Marrows come in green varieties, white varieties, and striped varieties (my favourites). No one else in Europe seems to touch them. I think they have gained huge popularity at country shows, where people compete for the biggest example, which seems a shame for the poor old marrow.

a few facts about courgettes

The courgette wasn't known in Europe before the voyages of Columbus. It seems it was the Italians who first marketed what is a baby marrow, since as late as the 1920s the

jan	feb	mar	apr	may	jun	jul	aug	sep	oct	nov	dec

French were still referring to courgettes as '*courges d'Italie*'. The fact we've adopted the French word 'courgette' rather than the Italian 'zucchini' indicates how late these veg arrived in Britain.

buying and storing courgettes

You don't want great big courgettes, which are becoming marrows, but neither do you want tiny ones, which have little flavour; they should be 7.5–12cm (3–5 inches) long. The skin should be glossy and blemish-free and the veg firm; you should not be able to bend it without snapping it. A courgette will last refrigerated for about 4 days.

preparing raw courgettes

Cut off the ends, then grate the courgette and add lemon juice and possibly mint.

boiling and steaming courgettes

Cut off the ends, then slice into thumb-widths. For boiling, bring a pan of salted water to the boil, plunge the veg in, and cook for 2 minutes; drain. For steaming, bring a pan of salted water to the boil and, when steam builds up, add the courgettes; sit the sieve over the water (it shouldn't touch it) and cook, lid on, for 4 minutes.
Try with: a tomato sauce.

frying courgettes

Cut off the ends, then slice into thumb-widths. Heat 1 tbsp of veg oil per 100g (3½oz) courgettes in a frying pan over a medium heat and fry for 2 minutes on each side.
Try with: minced beef.

griddling courgettes

Cut off the ends, then thinly slice the veg lengthways and brush both sides with olive oil. Heat the griddle pan. When hot, add the slices and cook for 1 minute on each side.
Try with: roasted veg.

frying courgette flowers in batter

Beat an egg and add it to 55g (2oz) of seasoned plain flour. Add enough cold water for a thin batter. Beat. Refrigerate for 1 hour. Heat a frying pan with a little olive oil over a high heat. When shimmering hot, dip the flower in the batter, add it to the pan and cook.
Try with: a sprinkling of salt and a pinch of freshly grated Parmesan.

courgette sauce for pasta

Pasta is so simple to cook, but trying to find good sauces is not so easy. This is very simple to make and repays your time beautifully with full flavours and a creamy texture.

serves 4

50g (1³/₄oz) butter

4 tbsp olive oil

2 cloves of garlic, finely sliced

1kg (2lb 4oz) courgettes, finely sliced

salt and black pepper

large handful of spaghetti

200g (7oz) scape, chopped

6 tbsp crème fraîche

50g (1³/₄oz) Parmesan, freshly grated, plus extra to serve

Melt the butter with the oil in a large pan over a medium heat.

Add the garlic, courgettes and seasoning. Cook gently for 20 minutes.

Bring a large pan of salted water to the boil. Cook the spaghetti according to the packet instructions, then drain well in a colander.

Add the scape, crème fraîche and Parmesan to the sauce and cook for a minute or so, stirring well.

Mix the sauce into the pasta and serve sprinkled with Parmesan,

courgette and radish salad

When you have taken the trouble to source good ingredients, I recommend doing as little to them as you possibly can.

serves 4

bunch of radishes, cut into julienne strips (matchsticks)

125g (4¹/₂oz) small courgettes, cut into julienne strips

salt and black pepper

2 tbsp sherry vinegar

¹/₂ tsp salt

1 tsp Dijon mustard

pinch of caster sugar

1 tbsp finely chopped dill

6 tbsp olive oil

Season the radish and courgette juliennes with salt and pepper.

Using a small whisk, whisk together the vinegar, salt, mustard, sugar and dill. Add the olive oil, beating all the time.

Toss the vegetables in the dressing and serve.

courgette and potato frittata

I love frittatas. They're light, fluffy and packed with goodies. Their ability to carry so many varied tastes and textures makes them an essential part of anybody's kitchen repertoire. The courgette sits happily in this dish, adding to its flavour and colour, but you need to extract moisture from them or else they will make the frittata soggy.

serves 6

225g (8oz) courgettes

salt and black pepper

25g (1oz) butter

2 tbsp olive oil

2 cloves of garlic,
finely chopped

bunch of spring onions,
finely chopped

10 eggs

10 grates of nutmeg

60g (2¹/₄oz) Parmesan,
freshly grated

1 tbsp chopped parsley

2 tsp chopped mint leaves

225g (8oz) salad potatoes,
cooked and quartered

Top and tail the courgettes, then grate them and place them in a sieve. Salt them heavily and leave for 20 minutes. Rinse under a cold tap and squeeze the flesh against the side of the sieve. Pat the pulp dry with kitchen towel.

Melt the butter with 1 tbsp of the oil in a frying pan over a low heat. Add the garlic, spring onions and grated courgette. Fry gently for 10 minutes; you only want a light colouring. Remove the mixture from the pan, but don't wash the pan.

Meanwhile, crack the eggs into a large, clean bowl. Add the nutmeg and Parmesan and beat well. Add the parsley, mint, the veg you have just fried and the salad potatoes.

Heat the remaining oil in the pan you used before. Carefully pour in the frittata mixture. Cook gently for about 5 minutes; the base or bottom of the frittata needs to be firm.

When the whole thing moves as one but the top is still a wet raw mix, place under a medium grill until the top firms – approximately 10 minutes. Remove the pan just as the last liquid sets. If you leave it to cook for longer you have not created a frittata, you've made a Frisbee.

courgette and lamb patties

This is a great recipe for kids as well as grown-ups. My two children, Tom and Libby, helped with the mixing.

serves 6

500g (1lb 2oz) courgettes, grated

salt and black pepper

500g (1lb 2oz) minced lamb

2 tbsp finely chopped dill

1 onion, grated

60g (2¼oz) cream cheese

2 eggs, beaten

2 tbsp plain flour

2 tbsp olive oil

Place the grated courgette in a sieve, sprinkle with salt and let it drain for 30 minutes. Rinse under a cold tap, then squeeze the flesh against the side of the sieve and dry on kitchen towel.

Combine the courgette, lamb, dill, onion, cream cheese, beaten eggs and some some black pepper. Mix in the flour and form 12 burger-shaped patties.

Heat the olive oil in a frying pan and fry the patties over a medium heat for about 5–10 minutes on each side, until golden brown and cooked through.

marrow stuffed with mince

I'm a big fan of minced beef as well as of marrow. The marrow gives a slight, but pleasing, firmness to the palate. It also acts as a cleansing agent for the sticky mince. This is a dish best enjoyed with a glass of slightly chilled cider.

serves 6

4 tbsp sunflower oil

2 cloves of garlic, crushed

2 onions, chopped

500g (1lb 2oz) minced beef

1 beef stock cube

400g tin chopped tomatoes

salt and black pepper

1 marrow

55g (2oz) Parmesan, freshly grated

Heat the oil in a pan over a medium heat, then cook the garlic and onion, stirring, for about 7 minutes, until the onion is soft. Add the mince and cook until the mince has colour, about 5 minutes.

Add the stock cube to 600ml (1 pint) of boiling water and add this to the mince. Add the tomatoes. Heavily season with salt and pepper and bring to the boil. Reduce the heat and simmer, lid off, for 1½ hours, or until the liquid has reduced, giving an almost jam-like texture (like shepherd's pie).

Preheat the oven to 200°C/400°F/gas mark 6.

Lightly top and tail the marrow. Cut it in half lengthways. With a spoon, hollow out a deep, wide groove in the marrow halves; don't split the sides or go up to the edges.

Fill the marrow halves with the mince and bake for 30 minutes. Sprinkle Parmesan on top and cook for another 10 minutes.

fennel

I get through a fair amount of fennel at home.
I loved Black Jack sweets when I was a kid, and
that aniseed flavour got stuck in my subconscious,
which is probably why I love fennel now. In fact,
I'm quite partial to a drop of Pernod, too. This slight
aniseed flavour makes fennel a perfect, and very
clean, accompaniment for white fish. However, if
you're lucky enough to find fennel with a large fern
or fronds, then cook these fronds with the fish
instead of the bulb; you'll get an even more subtle,
although noticeable, aniseed flavour.

Fennel is actually a member of the parsley family. It is a versatile beauty. It can be sliced or grated and eaten raw, fried, steamed, roasted and braised. Raw fennel is a stunningly good salad item: crunch, juice and loads of flavour. And the seeds are perfectly edible and transplant their flavour if used as a herb or spice.

types of fennel

Fennel has a sex: the tall flat one is male, the bulbous one female. You can get **bitter fennel**, **sweet fennel** and **Florence fennel** – the latter is what you want for veg. I was really excited when we got our first fennel seeds at the farm, but unfortunately we'd bought the bitter stuff, and I ended up with half a greenhouse full of long, inedible, lime-green shoots, with more fronds than you've ever seen! To start off with, the London chefs I sold to seemed quite pleased to buy a bag of fennel fronds, but by the end of the season they were fed up with the stuff. Sweet fennel is also used mostly for the flavouring gained from its seeds and leaves.

a few facts about fennel

Fennel has been used in Europe since the beginning of the classical era as a seed for flavouring and as a vegetable. Greek mythology would have us believe that Prometheus stole fire from the gods and hid it in the hollow stalk of a fennel bulb. The Romans were great lovers of fennel, and it makes many an appearance in Roman literature. Charlemagne ordered it to be grown in the south of France in the 9th century. Fennel must have come to Britain from Italy, and the first records of it being grown here are from the early 18th century. The word 'fennel' originates from the Latin for 'hay'.

buying fennel

Look for bulbs with the fern or fronds intact. A healthy frond is the sign of a just-picked fennel bulb. Make sure none of the arms are broken or the bulb cut in any way, and check the very tips of these arms, as they discolour and turn brown with age.

storing fennel

Fennel will keep very well in the fridge for up to a week.

| jan | feb | mar | apr | may | jun | jul | aug | sep | oct | nov | dec |

preparing raw fennel

Cut off the arms of the fennel and trim off the base. Slice on a mandolin. Add a squeeze of lemon juice – this stops the fennel from turning brown – but note that it will start to cook the fennel, softening it and turning it transparent. The stringy texture of fennel means it's not good for grating.

Try with: a salad.

cooking with fennel fronds (leaf)

The slight aniseed of the fronds is perfect for white fish. When you cook whole fish or fillets in foil, add plenty of fennel fronds to the parcel. It also adds to the flavour as well as the look of a fish soup or broth.

Try with: a salad – raw fennel fronds look stunning against the red of a tomato.

braising fennel

Preheat the oven to 180°C/350°F/gas mark 4. Cut off the arms of the fennel, trim off the base and cut the bulb into quarters. Heat 2 tbsp of vegetable oil per 100g (3½oz) of fennel in a pan. When the oil is hot, add the fennel and cook, turning, for 4 minutes to soften the fennel and give it colour. Place the fennel in a baking dish. Add a clove of crushed garlic and 2 tbsp of white wine vinegar per 100g (3½oz) of fennel and cover with chicken stock. Cover the dish with foil. Cook for 35 minutes, or until very soft.

Try with: any white fish or chicken.

cooking fennel in cream

Preheat the oven to 180°C/350°F/gas mark 4. Cut off the arms of the fennel, trim off the base and cut the bulb into quarters. Heat 2 tbsp of vegetable oil per 100g (3½oz) of fennel in a pan. When the oil is hot, add the fennel and cook, turning, for 4 minutes to soften the fennel and give it colour. Place the fennel in a baking dish. Add a clove of crushed garlic and cover with double cream. Cover the dish with foil. Cook the fennel for 35 minutes, or until very soft. A couple of minutes before the end of the cooking time, add 1 tsp of chopped dill, cover the dish and finish cooking in the oven.

Try with: any white fish, chicken or pork.

pan-frying fennel

Cut off the arms of the fennel and trim off the base. Slice on a mandolin. Heat 2 tbsp of vegetable oil per 100g (3½oz) of fennel in a frying pan over a medium heat. When the oil is hot add a knob of butter – about 10g (¼oz). Instantly add the fennel slices. Turn down the heat to low and cook the slices for 2 minutes on each side – you want it to be soft but not brown, only slight colour accepted here!
Try with: fish goujons and tartare sauce.

steaming fennel

Cut off the arms of the fennel and trim off the base. Cut off the fronds and keep to one side. Slice the fennel on a mandolin. Put the fronds and fennel slices in a sieve. Bring a pan of salted water to the boil and wait for a good amount of steam to build up before adding the fennel. Sit the sieve over the pan of boiling water – ensure it does not touch the water – and cover with a lid. Cook for 15 minutes.
Try with: any meat or white fish.

stir-frying fennel

Cut off the arms of the fennel and trim off the base. Slice on a mandolin. Heat 2 tbsp of sesame oil per 100g (3½oz) of fennel in a wok. When the oil is hot, add half a clove of finely sliced garlic. Sizzle for 20 seconds, then throw the fennel in and cook, stirring, for 3 minutes.
Try with: other stir-fried ingredients of your choice.

mussels in white wine with fennel

This is a take on moules marinières. Fennel and fish, any fish, make a great combination.

serves 4

salt and black pepper

2 large bulbs of fennel, trimmed, sliced and cut into matchsticks

1.8kg (4lb) mussels, scrubbed and beards removed

175ml (6fl oz) white wine

2 sprigs of thyme

25g (1oz) butter

4 shallots, finely chopped

1 clove of garlic, crushed

175ml (6fl oz) single cream

2 tbsp cornflour

1 tbsp finely chopped parsley

1 tbsp finely chopped dill

Bring a pan of salted water to the boil. Drop in the fennel matchsticks and boil, lid off, for about 5 minutes, until tender. Drain in a colander.

Discard any mussels that are damaged or do not close when tapped against the side of the sink. Put them into a large pan and add 100ml (3½fl oz) of water, 85ml (3fl oz) of the white wine and the thyme. Cover with a tightly fitting lid, bring to the boil, cover and cook for 5 minutes, or until the mussels are open, shaking the pot from time to time.

Drain the mussels, reserving the liquid and discarding any mussels that remain closed. When cool enough to handle, remove the mussels from the shells.

Melt the butter in a pan over a medium heat. Add the shallots and garlic and fry for 4–5 minutes, until softened. Add the fennel and fry for another minute. Pour in the mussel cooking liquor plus the remaining white wine and simmer gently until the liquid has reduced by half. Add the single cream.

Blend the cornflour with a little water of the cooking water and add it to the pan with the mussels, parsley and dill. Stir for 5 minutes or so, season well and serve.

fennel and tomato salad

I love pure food like this. The sweetness of good tomatoes and the aniseed of fennel taste great together.

serves 4

4 bulbs of fennel

juice of 2 lemons

100ml (3½fl oz) extra virgin olive oil

10 plum tomatoes

black pepper

Remove the fronds from the fennel and put them to one side. Cut off the green arms and trim off the base.

Pour the lemon juice and oil into a clean bowl.

Slice the fennel very thinly and put the slices in a bowl, adding some of the oil and lemon dressing as you go. This will stop the fennel discolouring and it will slightly cook and soften the fennel.

Slice the tomatoes and arrange them on a plate. Spoon the fennel into the centre of the plate and sprinkle some of the fronds on the top. Grind over some black pepper and serve with bread.

garlic

Garlic is an allium, which means it is a member of the onion family. Like most alliums, garlic forms a skin around its bulbs as it ages, and as this skin dries and toughens it becomes almost like paper, creating protective layers over the bulbs so that the flesh stays fine as long as it is firm. However, between May and August you may find new, young or fresh garlic. It is easily identifiable to the touch, as the skin remains wet and slippery. The bulbs underneath are incredibly mild and, with a little roasting, can be spread straight on to toast. I love it.

Garlic is a basic and important ingredient in cuisines all over the world, from the Indian sub-continent through China to southern and now most of Europe. It is ubiquitous but usually almost invisible in a dish, so I suspect many of us enjoyed it before we realized what it was. Garlic took a long time to gain acceptance in Britain. I can remember, as a kid, my dad and grand-dad complaining bitterly that the pie they'd ordered in a café had garlic in it. To them garlic was, like snails, something people ate on the Continent.

I think garlic made inroads into the British psyche through our love of curries and Elizabeth David's writings about Mediterranean cooking. In the late 1960s and early 1970s my mum and her working-class mates thought garlic was terribly sophisticated.

I don't like garlic presses – any cook worth his salt should be able to crush, chop or slice garlic without one. They are quick, but they are also hard to clean. I advocate using salt to help crush garlic; those tough little grains help break down the bulbs, and at the same time absorb the juices and are slightly abrasive to your chopping board, stopping the juices getting into the board and cleaning it at the same time.

Garlic, when cooked, will infuse into any other flavour. The longer you cook it for, the milder it will get. A raw clove sliced and then rubbed around the inside of a salad bowl will give a subtle but pleasant flavour. Also, the smaller you chop it the stronger the flavour will be, so if you want a very mild flavour cook the cloves whole, for the next step up chop them, and for the most flavour crush them. Garlic does taint and stay on the breath, but chewing parsley will help take that smell away.

types of garlic

The thing to consider, when choosing garlic, is its condition rather than variety. In the summer, look out for new-season, wet-skinned garlic. Garlic gets more bitter as it gets older (careful cooking can take this away). Garlic skin is usually white, but it can come with a pink or purple tint. I have heard people say the purple is best, but for the life of me I've never understood why. **Scape** is the tendrils that grow off garlic plants; they curl up like a pig's tail. They taste good added to a dish with herbs or finely chopped and stir-fried.

jan	feb	mar	apr	may	jun	jul	aug	sep	oct	nov	dec

a few facts about garlic

We get the word 'garlic' from the Anglo Saxon 'gar leac', meaning spear-shaped plant. It is widely believed that the Romans first brought garlic to Britain, but it fell out of favour in the 'Dark Ages' and was popularized again, at least in the rest of Europe if not Britain, by the Crusaders returning from the Holy Lands. We do have evidence of garlic from Picardy being sold in London markets in the 13th century, so it seems it's been with us for a long time but, until recently, not very popular.

Garlic may have become unpopular after the Henrician Reformation. To the new Protestants garlic, which was mostly grown in the hot south of Europe, could have represented Spain, France and Papism. John Evelyn, a self-confessed vegetable lover, referred to its 'intolerable rankness'. As late as the Victorian era, Mrs Beeton was warning that it 'will taint the breath' and she suggested boiling it very well.

Garlic, medicine and paganism are intertwined like no other food. Garlic has long been considered to ward off vampires. In Romania, it was once widely worn as an amulet to ward off the evil eye. The ancient Greeks put garlic at crossroads to keep Hecate, the goddess of the underworld, happy. Garlic was used as a medicine in Egypt from 1,550BC and in India from around 5,000 years ago. Throughout history garlic has been used to treat animal bites, particularly snake bites, and many open wounds. As late as the First World War, British doctors used garlic as an antiseptic.

buying garlic

Never buy garlic that has green sprouts (if it sprouts once you've got it home, cut the green off). Bulbs should be firm. White, pinkish or purple-tinted skins are all fine.

storing garlic

The papery skin that envelopes each clove, and then a second skin that embraces the whole, is a perfect natural protection, which means garlic stored in cool and airy conditions will last for several weeks.

raw garlic

Rubbing a whole garlic clove around a dish you are cooking with will give a dish just a hint of garlic. To step up the flavour, rub the food – in particular a joint of meat — with the garlic. If you're going to use raw garlic in salads, you really need fresh garlic, so use it in season. By the time the skin is papery the bulb is too bitter.
Try with: salads; new season's garlic is also perfect in marinades or aïoli (see page 101).

slicing, chopping and crushing garlic

The legendary Michel Roux senior taught me to always slice a garlic clove in half and then remove the root. With younger garlic the root appears as a thin white line; as the garlic ages this white line gets thicker and more pronounced, and it eventually turns green, getting more and more bitter all the time. Many a cook has incorrectly deduced they have burnt their garlic, when it's the bitter root that's the problem. Whether you slice, chop or crush a clove will depend on how strong a garlic flavour you want – the more finely chopped the garlic, the more flavour it will impart to the dish, so crushing gives maximum flavour. After the root has gone, sprinkle salt on the clove halves. For crushing, lay a big knife over them, positioning the garlic as near to the knife handle as you can, and make sure the sharp blade of the knife is pointed down towards the chopping board at an 80° angle. Hold the knife handle with one hand and carefully smack the knife with the other, keeping your hand away from the sharp edge of the blade. Still holding the handle of the knife, put the blade edge over the garlic. Holding the blunt edge of the blade in your hand, with your fingers gripping the blade near the sharp end, scrape the sharp blade across the garlic bit by bit until it's flattened, starting with the bit of the garlic closest to you and working away from your body, until you have a paste.

frying garlic

Heat a little oil in a pan over a medium heat. Add crushed or finely chopped garlic and cook until golden, but never allow the garlic to brown as this means it's burnt – it will make the whole dish taste a bit like paraffin. If you do burn the garlic, throw everything away, especially the oil, and start again.

roasting or braising whole garlic cloves

Place the peeled garlic cloves beside meat or fish being roasted or braised. If the cooking smells tell you you're not getting enough garlic flavour, you can always crush them, or some of them, at any time in during cooking. Unfortunately, it's impossible to be taught when to do this; it's down to personal taste and comes with experience. Try with: roast chicken.

roasting a bulb of garlic

Preheat the oven to 180°C/350°F/gas mark 4. Put the garlic bulb, unpeeled, on a sheet of tin foil. Drizzle with 1 tbsp of olive oil. Wrap the foil around it, not tightly, to create a little bag. Roast for 45 minutes for fresh garlic; up to 1 hour for older garlic. Alternatively, with really fresh garlic, cut the top fifth off the garlic, put it on a roasting tray, drizzle 1 tbsp of olive oil over the cut surface, then put in the oven cut-surface uppermost and cook until the cut surface is brown, weeping and caramelized – roughly 30 minutes. Older garlic will not caramelize as well as the young.

Try: spread over toast.

stir-frying garlic

You can crush or thinly slice garlic for stir-frying – I don't recommend chopping it. Heat some sesame oil in a wok over a high heat. Add the garlic and sizzle for 20 seconds, stirring. When you add the garlic, make sure the rest of your ingredients are prepared and ready to cook so that you can cook everything quickly and not risk burning your garlic.

cooking scape

Scape is the tendrils that grow off garlic plants. The major difference between cooking scape and garlic cloves is the timing of adding it to a dish. Garlic cloves go in at the beginning of the cooking, scape goes in towards the end. I like it sliced finely in a salad or risotto, added at the end as with herbs, or finely chopped and stir-fried in a wok.

Try with: salads.

chicken with 40 cloves of roast garlic

Say no to roast chicken, say no to life. Don't let the amount of fresh herbs or garlic put you off this dish. Deep in the cavity they release subtle flavour. Testimonial of my garlic chicken comes from the educated palate of my girlfriend, Amanda. Arriving at my flat as the bird was resting, she demolished a wing and a leg as I was washing my hands.

1 x 1.5kg (3lb 5oz) chicken
salt
1 tbsp thyme leaves
1 tbsp chopped rosemary
1 tbsp chopped parsley
4 bay leaves
40 cloves of garlic, unpeeled
½ lemon
4 tbsp olive oil

Preheat the oven to 200°C/400°F/gas mark 6.

Rinse the chicken under cold water, then pat it dry with kitchen towel. Rub salt into the skin.

Stuff the cavity with half the herbs, 10 garlic cloves and the lemon. Put the chicken in a roasting tin.

Scatter the rest of the garlic and herbs around the chicken. Drizzle the oil over everything.

Roast in the oven, basting every 20 minutes, for 90 minutes, or until the chicken is cooked through.

roast new season garlic on croûtons

This is lovely. Even now, as I'm typing, I want to go back into the kitchen and make some more. Eat it with your fingers; everybody loves to.

serves 4
4 fat bulbs of new-season garlic
4 tbsp olive oil
16 thin slices of French bread
garlic cream cheese, to serve

Preheat the oven to 180°C/350°F/gas mark 4.

Cut the tops off the garlic bulbs so you can see the cloves. Place them in a small roasting tin, cut surface up, drizzle with olive oil and roast for about 30 minutes, until brown and caramelized.

Towards the end of the cooking time, heat some olive oil in a frying pan over a medium heat. Add the slices of French bread and fry until crisp and lightly browned. Keep warm.

Serve each garlic bulb with the croûtons, placing a bowl of garlic cream cheese on the table. Squeeze the garlic from the cooked cloves like toothpaste on to the croûtons.

leeks

These beauties are alliums, which makes them part of the onion family. They have the unmistakeable smell and sharpness of an onion, but are far milder and less sweet. I'm a big fan of leeks. I find them easier to use than onions; they're not wet and slippery when peeled and, more importantly, they don't make your eyes red and your nose run. I'm not sure if people realise that when a recipe calls for an onion, it can usually be replaced with a leek. I like to think of the leek as a subtle, mature member of the allium family.

Abergavenny in South Wales holds a very fine annual food festival. When I'm there, being a greengrocer among the Welsh, the conversation often turns to leeks. I've heard many a Welshman say that the green of the leek resembles the lush Welsh valleys and the white part the top of the mountains. I reply that they are indeed fortunate to have found a vegetable that matches their environment. As a passionate Londoner, I'm always on the lookout for a grey vegetable covered in graffiti.

Leeks have been popular for as long as I've been a greengrocer, but I have no choice but to believe Jane Grigson when she says that 'they only gained popularity in the last 30 years'. Jane's theory is that a lack of running water in the cities, and the difficulty of cleaning the leek without it, relegated the veg to a bit player.

Indeed the cleaning of leeks is their only drawback. The reason for this is that once leeks strengthen, the earth around them is piled up to 'blanch' them. Keeping a leek hidden from the sun ensures whiter and milder flesh. The longer and whiter the stem, the more tender it will be. The green becomes coarse and bitter.

types of leeks

The leek comes in a range of sizes. Always tubular in appearance, they vary from pencil thin to nearly as wide as your leg. Huge ones are much loved by people who grow and show, and very silly it is to have a leek as big as your leg!

Obviously, baby leeks are immature, but that's only half the story. Once they have seeded and are sprouting, leeks are usually thinned out to allow room for the bigger healthier shoots to grow (this happens with many vegetables). Baby leeks aren't thinned, so they would struggle to grow as they must share nutrients and space with brothers and sisters. Small baby leeks are among my favourite vegetables – they are packed with flavour and haven't developed many layers for dirt to hide in.

Some Middle Eastern recipes call for green leeks, but don't cook with the green part of the leek you have. Middle Eastern leeks have been bred to have a milder, smoother green than the European ones.

a few facts about leeks

Leeks were cultivated by the ancient Egyptians. The Romans believed them to be superior to the onion, which they felt was only fit for the poor. The Emperor Nero

jan	feb	mar	apr	may	jun	jul	aug	sep	oct	nov	dec

was reported to have eaten leeks daily; he believed they would enhance his singing voice. He was given the nickname '*porrophagus*' meaning 'leek-eater' in Latin.

The leek is the national emblem of Wales. Legend has it that when a Welsh king was due to fight a battle with the incoming Saxons, he ordered his men to wear leeks ion their hats to tell friend from foe. The Welsh were victorious, and adopted the leek.

buying and storing leeks

Leeks should be bought with the green crisscross leaves intact and the crossing should be firm. The white should be wrinkle-free and smooth. Try to buy leeks as thin as possible; fat ones have a tendency to develop hard, long shards through the centre to support that enormous weight. Leeks will sit happily in the fridge for up to a week.

preparing raw leeks

Leeks need careful cleaning. Cut off all but 5cm (2 inches) of the green tops and trim off the roots. Remove a layer if necessary. If using whole, cut through the middle to within 3cm (1¼ inches) of the root end, but don't cut right through. Wash well under a running cold tap, fanning the layers to ensure all grit is removed. If not cooking whole, chop into suitable bits and wash very well under a running tap. Drain well in a colander.

cooking leeks in butter or cream

Bring a pan of salted water to the boil. Add the whole leeks and boil for 8–10 minutes. Drain, squeezing. Heat a knob of butter in a pan, add the leeks and 2 tbsp of veg stock and cook, lid off, over a high heat for 3 minutes, until the liquid has evaporated. Season. For cream, once the stock has almost evaporated add single cream and dill and stir. Try with: pork chops for butter, roast chicken for cream.

puréeing leeks

Slice the leeks thinly. Heat a knob of butter in a pan over a medium heat, add the leeks, season and cook, lid on, for 8–10 minutes. If there is any liquid left, boil hard until it evaporates. Transfer to a processor, add a little single cream and nutmeg and purée. Try with: lamb.

cooking baby leeks

Prepare as for large leeks. As baby leeks are so cute and tasty, cook them whole as either buttered or creamed above. You need a shorter cooking time as they are smaller.

baby leeks and béarnaise sauce

Once you can make béarnaise sauce, you will find making hollandaise easy, too. While I find a béarnaise a little too powerful for a steak, the juice in a baby leek seems to dilute the acidity of the sauce. A baby leek on its own could be accused of being dull, but it certainly isn't when eaten with a good sauce.

serves 4

28 baby leeks, trimmed

80g (2³/₄oz) shallots, thinly sliced

25g (1oz) roughly chopped tarragon

10 tbsp white wine vinegar

2 egg yolks

125g (4¹/₂oz) butter, melted

Cut the leeks into 15–20cm (6–8 inch) lengths.

Put the shallots, tarragon and vinegar in a pan. Bring to the boil, then simmer for 15 minutes. Strain and keep the liquor.

Bring a pan of salted water to the boil and add the leeks. Boil for 4 minutes, then drain.

Put the egg yolks in a bowl and whisk with an electric whisk until the mixture doubles in size. Add the shallot liquor and whisk. Gradually pour in the butter, constantly whisking. If it curdles, add 1 tbsp of warm water.

Serve the leeks with the béarnaise poured over them.

leeks, peas and haddock baked in a bag

Dishes like this, that are served in their own little tin-foil bag, seem to really impress dinner guests. This is tasty and easy to make.

serves 4

60g (2¹/₄oz) butter

1 tbsp vegetable oil

8 baby leeks, trimmed and thinly sliced

300g (10¹/₂oz) podded peas

8 tbsp white wine

4 tsp chopped dill

salt and black pepper

4 x 150g (5¹/₂oz) pieces of haddock fillet, skinned

Preheat the oven to 190°C/375°F/gas mark 5. Cut out 4 squares of kitchen foil, each big enough to hold the fish and veg.

Melt the butter with the vegetable oil in a pan over a medium heat. Add the leeks and peas, and sweat, lid on, for 10 minutes.

Add the white wine, dill and seasoning to taste and simmer until the liquid has evaporated.

Put a quarter of the vegetables in the middle of each piece of foil. Top with a piece of haddock and season. Fold over the foil to make a loose, but tightly sealed, parcel. Put the parcels on a baking sheet and bake for 30 minutes. Open the parcels carefully on a serving plate.

Welsh eggs

This is a take on Scotch eggs. Trying to pack the mixture around the hard-boiled egg does seem tricky at first, but my advice is to try it with a friend after you have both downed the best part of a bottle of good white Burgundy!

serves 4

6 eggs, hard-boiled for
7 minutes and cooled under
cold water

3 tbsp plain flour, seasoned

2 tbsp vegetable oil, plus extra
for deep-frying

1 leek, trimmed and finely
chopped

115g (4oz) fresh white
breadcrumbs

grated zest and juice of 1 lemon

50g (1³/₄oz) shredded suet

2 tbsp chopped parsley

1 tbsp thyme leaves

1 tbsp chopped chives

salt and black pepper

1 egg

80g (2³/₄oz) dried breadcrumbs

Peel the hard-boiled eggs and roll them in the seasoned flour. Put to one side.

Heat the vegetable oil in a frying pan over a medium heat. Add the leek and fry gently for 2–4 minutes, until softened. Remove from the heat and leave to cool.

Combine the leek with the fresh breadcrumbs, lemon zest and juice, suet, herbs and seasoning to taste. If the mixture is dry, add a little water.

Shape the mixture around the hard-boiled eggs, moulding it firmly with your hands.

Beat the egg in a large bowl. Roll each egg first in the beaten egg, then in the dried breadcrumbs. Chill in the fridge for 30 minutes.

Heat the oil for deep-frying in a heavy-based pan or deep-fat fryer to 190°C/375°F. Test to see if it is ready by dropping in some breadcrumbs; if they sizzle it is ready. Carefully place 3 of the chilled eggs in the hot oil and cook for about 3 minutes, until they are brown. Cook the remaining eggs in the same way. Drain very well on kitchen towel. Serve cool.

leeks baked with ham in a cheese sauce

Be sure that your paprika is very fresh for this recipe. This recipe is close to my heart as I play and coach rugby at London Welsh.

serves 4

25g (1oz) butter, plus extra for greasing

salt and black pepper

8 leeks (not too large), trimmed

8 large thin slices of cooked ham

250ml (9fl oz) crème fraîche

100g (3½oz) mature Cheddar, grated

pinch of cayenne pepper

1 tsp Dijon mustard

Preheat the oven to 190°C/375°F/gas mark 5. Grease a gratin dish.

Bring a large pan of salted water to the boil. Add the leeks and boil, lid off, for 15 minutes. Drain the leeks thoroughly in a colander, saving 4 tbsp of the cooking water. When cooled, squeeze the leeks slightly with your hands.

Wrap each leek in a slice of ham and place it, seam-side down, in the gratin dish. Season to taste with salt and black pepper.

In a bowl, mix together the crème fraîche, reserved cooking water, half the Cheddar, the cayenne and Dijon mustard. Pour the mixture over the leeks.

Sprinkle over the rest of the cheese and bake for about 30 minutes, until golden.

vichyssoise

You all know vichyssoise, don't you? If you want to make it, simply follow this recipe.
I mean, just look down at how easy it is.

serves 4

60g (2¹/₄oz) butter

3 large leeks, trimmed
and sliced

1 onion, finely chopped

2 potatoes, chopped into 5cm
(2 inch) dice

1.2 litres (2 pints) vegetable
or chicken stock

salt and black pepper

150ml (5¹/₂fl oz) single cream

2 tbsp finely chopped chives,
to garnish

Melt the butter in a large pan over a medium heat. Add the leeks
and onion, and sweat, lid on, for 15 minutes.

Add the potatoes and stock, and season to taste. Bring to the boil,
cover, reduce the heat and simmer for about 20 minutes, until the
potatoes are tender.

Whiz with a hand-held blender, then pass through a sieve. Chill for
at least 3 hours.

To serve, stir in the cream and season again, if necessary. Spoon
into individual bowls and garnish with chives.

cock-a-leekie

Just the mention of this dish makes me want to don a kilt and eat in a large hall!
Boy, is this dish good.

serves 6

1 x 1.5kg (3lb 5oz) chicken

1 onion, quartered

2 carrots, chopped

8 black peppercorns

2 sprigs parsley, with stalks

1 bouquet garni

salt and black pepper

25g (1oz) butter

6 leeks, trimmed and thinly
sliced

2 spring onions, trimmed and
thinly sliced

6 ready-to-eat prunes

2 tbsp finely chopped parsley

Place the chicken, onion, carrots, peppercorns, parsley, bouquet
garni and 1 tsp of salt in a large pan. Cover with water, place on a
medium heat and bring to the boil slowly. Cover with a tight-fitting
lid and simmer for 1 hour, skimming off any white scum. Check
the chicken is immersed in water throughout cooking; top it up
with boiling water if necessary.

Check the chicken is cooked by piercing the thigh with a skewer; if
the juices run clear then the chicken is done; if there is any pink it
needs longer. Remove the chicken when it is cooked and reserve.
Discard the veg and bits and pieces, but keep the stock. When the
bird is cool, remove the skin and cut the meat into thin strips.

Melt the butter in a large pan over a medium heat. Add the leeks
and spring onions and sweat, lid on, for 10 minutes. Add the
reserved stock and the prunes and simmer, lid on, for 15 minutes.
Add the chicken and simmer for 10 minutes. Stir in the parsley.

mushrooms

This book only looks at cultivated mushrooms –
after all, I am a greengrocer and cultivated veg
are what I trade in! I do enjoy wild mushrooms,
but these little critters can fill a book on their own.
Some wild mushrooms have been cultivated
successfully; I'm thinking in particular of oyster and
shiitake. But the best examples have been impossible
to farm; a lot of them have a complex relationship
with trees. We Brits love mushrooms, and eat them
for breakfast, dinner and tea. Whether it's mushroom
soup, mushrooms on toast or a warming chicken
and mushroom pie, we can find good use for them.

types of mushroom

The 3 most popular mushrooms are actually just 1 variety: **button**, **cup** and **flat** are all stages of development of the same mushroom.

Button is the youngest of the bunch. Its head has just popped through the earth and it has hardly any stem. The cap is very soft and it can be eaten raw, but it has hardly any flavour. **Closed cup** is the next stage on – the adolescent. It's a bigger mushroom than the button, around the size of a golf ball. Next comes the **open cup**. If you turn this mushroom upside down, you will notice the gills are developing and turning a pinky brown. These, cooks assure me, are perfect for stuffing (though why anybody would want to stuff a mushroom is beyond me). For properly grown-up mushrooms that are big in size and in flavour, you want **flat** (**field**).

The **Portobello** is the daddy of the cultivated mushroom. Big and beefy, it really does get close to tasting of beef. This is what you want on your breakfast plate. **Chestnut** mushrooms are immature Portobello mushrooms. But because the Portobello is bursting with meaty flavour, even while it is in the chestnut stage, it still tastes good – in fact, probably better than any cultivated mushroom of its size.

Oyster mushrooms were originally wild, but are now cultivated. In their wild state, they can be found on dead tree stumps. They get their name from their colour; it has nothing to do with their flavour. They have a lovely curved, alien-like appearance, being round of head and thin of stem. They contain a lot of moisture and will reduce right down when cooked. They don't have a huge amount of flavour; I'd rather have a flat mushroom any day. You can now get oysters in pink or yellow hues, but I'm not really a pretty mushroom man. **Shiitake** mushrooms were originally wild Chinese mushrooms, but have now been cultivated for many years in England.

a few facts about mushrooms

There is no mention of the term 'mushroom' in English until the 9th century. The smart money is on the name springing from the French *mousseron*. Now, of course, that French name is used for one type of mushroom. The book *Grete Herball* of 1526 refers to them as '*mussherons*'. I like this; I wish we still called them that. Mind you, it went on to say that most of them suffocate and strangle the eater. I can't believe this referred to a button or cup; it must be about some poisonous fungi lurking in the woods!

| jan | feb | mar | apr | may | jun | jul | aug | sep | oct | nov | dec |

The Greeks and Romans both cultivated mushrooms in classical times, but it seems more as a hobby than an industry. The scant evidence we have seems to point to wild varieties being grown by them on logs in gardens. The Chinese certainly used the log method probably much earlier than the Greeks and Romans.

Cultivation on a bigger scale is French in origin. Olivier de Serres catalogued his methods as early as the 17th century. From this point, mushroom-farming in France progressed rapidly, most of it centring around Paris. To this day, the cup-shaped standard mushroom of France is known as *champignon de Paris*.

buying mushrooms

Firmness is important in a mushroom – ensure there is no sponginess. Where possible, turn the mushroom upside down and look at its gills; these should be dry and firm.

storing mushrooms

As soon as you get your mushrooms home, take them out of the plastic bag or box; the plastic can cause condensation and make your mushrooms go soggy. Put them instead in a paper bag, then refrigerate them. They will be happy for up to 4 days.

preparing mushrooms

The big mushroom debate is about cleaning them. Some chefs say you should wash them, but *Larousse Gastronomique* recommends brushing them. My advice is to experiment. You could brush them with a very soft brush (don't drive yourself mad, you will be unlikely to brush off all the dirt), or you could wash them, but be careful. Hold your mushroom and just dunk it in the cold water, like you would a biscuit in a cup of tea, then dry with a paper towel. If the mushroom spends too long under water it will get waterlogged. The third suggestion falls somewhere between the two and is probably the best: simply wipe with a damp cloth. Look carefully for any damaged bits and trim these off along with the base of the stalks. Only peel the mushrooms if they are very discoloured.

cooking mushrooms in cream

Prepare and cook as for frying mushrooms (see page 178). Once the liquid has evaporated, add a little crème fraîche to taste.

Try: on toast.

grilling mushrooms

Use big flat mushrooms. Melt butter in a small pan. Heat the grill to medium–high. Brush the outer side of the mushrooms with melted butter, season and grill close to the heat for 5–7 minutes. Turn, brush the gill side with butter, season and grill for 5 minutes. Try with: steak.

frying mushrooms

Cut the prepared mushrooms into pieces if they are big. Melt a large knob of butter with a little vegetable oil in a frying pan over a high heat. When hot, add the mushrooms, season, and fry, uncovered, for 5–8 minutes, turning them once halfway through cooking, until the liquid has evaporated and the mushrooms are nice and brown. Try with: a fried breakfast.

roasting mushrooms

Cut the base off the stalks and clean the large flat mushrooms. Melt some butter in a frying pan and fry the mushrooms for 2–3 minutes. Transfer to a roasting dish and roast at 200°C/400°F/gas mark 6 for 10–15 minutes. Try with: fried bacon and grilled tomatoes.

roast field mushrooms with ham

The lemon juice is really important in this recipe, giving just the right amount of acidity to match the crème fraîche.

serves 4
8 large flat field mushrooms
60g (2¼oz) butter
2 shallots, finely chopped
125g (4½oz) cooked ham, finely chopped
4 tbsp crème fraîche
juice of ½ lemon
salt and black pepper

Preheat the oven to 200°C/400°F/gas mark 6.

Wipe the mushrooms with kitchen towel. Cut the bases from the mushroom stalks and discard. Cut off the stalks so they are level with the caps, and chop the stalks finely.

Melt the butter in a frying pan over a medium heat. Add the caps and cook them for 2–3 minutes on each side. Transfer the mushrooms to a roasting dish, all in one layer.

Return the frying pan to the heat and add the stalks and shallots. Fry until soft, about 5 minutes. Remove the pan from the heat and stir in the ham, crème fraîche and lemon juice.

Place the filling evenly over the mushrooms and season. Roast for 10–15 minutes.

flat mushrooms on toast

Try this and a pot of hot coffee for breakfast. For lunch, substitute the coffee for sparkling water. As a starter for dinner, swap the water for a decent white wine.

serves 4

400g (14oz) flat field mushrooms

40g (1¹/₂oz) butter

1 tbsp vegetable oil

4 tbsp crème fraîche

salt and black pepper

2 ciabatta rolls, halved and toasted

Wipe the mushrooms with kitchen towel, cut the bases from the stalks and discard, then cut the mushrooms into bite-size chunks.

Melt the butter with the oil in a wok or frying pan over a medium heat. Add the mushrooms. As soon as the mushrooms go in, increase the heat – mushrooms release a lot of liquid during cooking; we want them to fry, not boil, and turning up the heat will evaporate the liquid.

When the mushrooms are brown and not releasing any more liquid, remove the pan from the heat. Quickly stir in the crème fraîche and season. Serve on toasted ciabatta.

croissants stuffed with mushrooms

Croissants act as a wonderful vehicle for many different flavours.

serves 4

125g (4¹/₂oz) field mushrooms

25g (1oz) butter, plus extra for greasing

4 tbsp crème fraîche

1 tbsp medium-dry sherry

salt and pepper

12 easy-bake croissants

flour, for dusting

1 egg, beaten

Wipe the mushrooms, cut the bases from the stalks and discard, then chop the mushrooms finely. Preheat the oven as directed on the croissant pack. Grease a baking tray.

Melt the butter in a frying pan over a medium heat. Add the mushrooms and fry gently for about 4 minutes to soften, but do not allow to brown.

Add the crème fraîche and sherry and cook until any excess moisture has evaporated. Season to taste, remove from the heat and allow to cool.

Lay the croissant dough triangles on a lightly floured surface. Place a spoonful of the mushroom mixture at the wide end of the dough and brush the pointed end with beaten egg. Roll up, starting with the wide end, enclosing the filling.

Arrange the croissants on the baking tray and brush all over with beaten egg. Bake as per the pack instructions, until risen and golden brown. Serve warm.

chestnut mushroom risotto

Southern Italian food is my favourite, but the northern dish of risotto really is heavenly. The mushrooms have an almost meaty flavour, making them the perfect partner for the creamy rice.

serves 4

300g (10^1/$_2$oz) chestnut mushrooms
2 tbsp olive oil
1 onion, finely chopped
2 cloves of garlic, crushed
1 litre (1^3/$_4$ pints) chicken stock
250g (9oz) carnaroli rice
150ml (5fl oz) white wine
80g (2^3/$_4$oz) Parmesan, grated
55g (2oz) butter

Wipe the mushrooms with kitchen towel, cut the bases from the stalks and discard, then cut the mushrooms into quarters.

Heat 2 tbsp of the olive oil in a pan over a low heat. Add the mushrooms and cook, lid on, for 3 minutes. Drain the mushrooms, keeping the cooking liquor in a bowl.

Heat another 2 tbsp of olive oil in a second pan over a low heat. Add the onion and garlic and cook, stirring, for 2 minutes.

Meanwhile, heat the stock in a separate pan, then remove from the heat.

Add the rice to the onion and stir well. Add the white wine and keep stirring. Add a ladleful of stock and keep stirring. This is a labour of love; only add more stock, a ladleful at a time, after the rice has absorbed the last ladleful. This is the famous feast and famish method in making risotto.

When you have soft grains and a creamy texture (which could take 30 minutes), add the mushrooms and their liquor. Sprinkle over the Parmesan, stir it in and remove from the heat. Stir in the butter and serve.

chestnut mushroom soup

This is a lovely little soup and looks gorgeous served with a swirl of cream.

serves 4

300g (10¹/₂oz) chestnut mushrooms

50g (1³/₄oz) butter

1 shallot, finely chopped

350ml (12fl oz) full-fat milk

1 tbsp plain flour

1 tbsp chopped chives

salt and black pepper

8 tbsp single cream

Wipe the mushrooms, cut the bases from the stalks and discard. Slice the mushrooms thinly.

Melt half the butter in a large pan, then add the shallot and mushrooms. Cook gently, lid on, for 15 minutes, until tender.

Pass the mushrooms and shallots through a sieve, keeping the pulp and juice. This gives a better texture than puréeing. Make the mushroom juice up to 450ml (16fl oz) with milk.

Melt the remaining butter in a pan over a medium heat. Stir in the flour, then gradually add the mushroom and milk liquid, whisking to get a smooth soup. Add the mushroom pulp and the chives.

Season and stir in half the cream. Serve in bowls, swirling 1 tbsp of cream into each bowl for garnish.

lamb chops stuffed with mushrooms

This is not one for the faint-hearted, with its deep and meaty flavour.

serves 4

100g (3¹/₂oz) chestnut mushrooms

4 thick lamb chops, fat cut off

50g (1³/₄oz) butter

100g (3¹/₂oz) chicken livers, finely chopped

salt and black pepper

1 egg

50g (1³/₄oz) fresh wholemeal breadcrumbs

1 tbsp finely chopped parsley

Preheat the oven to 200°C/400°F/gas mark 6. Wipe the mushrooms, cut the bases from the stalks and discard, and finely chop the mushrooms.

Make a horizontal slit into the fattest part of each chop, so you can stuff it.

Melt half the butter in a frying pan over a medium heat. Add the chicken livers and mushrooms, and fry for about 5 minutes, until soft but not brown. Season and leave to cool slightly.

Spoon the mushroom stuffing into the lamb pockets. Secure the openings with cocktail sticks.

Beat the egg in a large bowl. On a plate, mix the breadcrumbs with some seasoning and the chopped parsley. Dip the chops into the egg, then the breadcrumbs. Put into a roasting tin. Melt the remaining butter and pour it over the chops. Bake for 15 minutes, turn over, then bake again for 15 minutes, until golden brown.

mushroom and chicken puff pastry pie

Chicken and mushroom is a classic combination, and this rich, satisfying pie shows the match off fantastically.

serves 4–6

butter, for greasing

1 x 900g (2lb) whole roast or poached chicken

300g (10¹/₂oz) mixed dark mushrooms, such as flat or chestnut

3 tbsp olive oil

5 tbsp plain flour

salt and black pepper

1 tsp roughly chopped tarragon

350ml (12fl oz) vegetable or chicken stock, or poaching liquid

6 tbsp double cream or crème fraîche

1 tbsp soy sauce

375g (13oz) ready-rolled puff pastry

1 egg, beaten

Preheat the oven to 220°C/425°F/gas mark 7. Grease a 1.75 litre (3 pint) pie dish.

Cut the cooked chicken into bite-size pieces and put the meat in the pie dish. Wipe the mushrooms, cut off the bases and discard, then slice the mushrooms thickly.

Heat half the olive oil in a frying pan over a medium to high heat. Fry the mushrooms for 3–4 minutes, turning once, until the liquid evaporates.

Add the rest of the oil along with the flour. Stir and season with salt, pepper and tarragon. Gradually pour in the stock, stirring, to make a thick sauce. Add the cream and soy, then pour the sauce over the chicken and stir.

Cut the pastry so it is the same shape as, but slightly larger than, the pie dish. From the remaining pastry, cut a long strip of pastry about 2cm (³/₄ inch) wide. Place this strip around the edge of the pie dish. Brush the rim with water and lift the pastry over the dish, pressing down firmly over the strip. Cut 2 slits in the top of the pastry. Trim the edges and brush the pastry with beaten egg.

Bake for about 30 minutes, until the pastry is golden.

onions and shallots

Where would we be without onions? How many recipes begin with 'take an onion'? In fact, the smell of onions frying in oil must be recognized the world over. I don't know anybody who doesn't like onions and I can't think of a country that doesn't grow them. They can be eaten raw, fried, boiled, braised, roasted or pickled. They feature heavily in all sorts of dishes – think of soups, stews, curries and chutneys. What other veg can claim such a rich heritage? Personally, I adore the smell of onions cooking. Whether it's hot or cold outside, as soon as I combine some chopped garlic and onion and add it to hot oil I'm in heaven.

The need to stir onions as they are softening and to keep a close eye on them in case they burn is no chore. My nose would happily sit above the pan all day. Onions cooking can make me hungry like no other food. I eat well, I shop hard and I like good food. But even now, at my age, I still find it difficult to walk past a street vendor, no matter how ghastly his burger or sausages appear. Onions, mmmmmm!

The onion is the daddy of the allium family. This extended family includes chives, garlic, leeks and shallots. There are, in fact, 500 species of alliums, and experts tell us these are a member of the lily family. I ask you, how can an onion be related to a lily?

Strangely, for such an enormously popular vegetable, the onion is not known as a wild plant. Still, it has played a major role in not only the cuisine, but also the mythology and medicine of all the world's major civilizations. What a boast!

When the subject of onions arises during my radio show, the conversation often turns to the subject of watery eyes and that awful burning sting that makes the chopping of an onion hazardous. These fumes are actually a sulphur compound and are the onion's defence mechanism. If you break the cells, this compound sprays into the air. It has kept most animals away from the onion throughout its history. There are many old wives' tales about how to avoid it, along the lines of 'onions without tears dear, yes, you have to chop them while standing on 3 porcupines and singing the national anthem in Greek'. Chopping onions under running water helps to wash away the compound, but quite how you finely chop an onion in the sink while holding on to it, I don't know. My advice is to suck a spoon. Honestly, I am not having you on. That sucking action actually closes your tear ducts.

I am obviously not the only holder of a British passport in love with his onions. Despite growing a very healthy 48,000 tonnes of the blighters every year, we are the world's biggest importer, bringing in an enormous 200,000 tonnes. To give you some idea of how big the onion market is, in 1998 (the last time, I think, a survey was done), the world was growing an estimated 39 million tonnes of onions, with China (the biggest grower) growing an impressive 10 million tonnes.

onions

jan	feb	mar	apr	may	jun	jul	aug	sep	oct	nov	dec

spring onions

jan	feb	mar	apr	may	jun	jul	aug	sep	oct	nov	dec

varieties of onion

Here are the major varieties of onions (for shallots, see below). The **bulb onion** is the common brown-skinned variety. The rule of thumb here is that generally the smaller they are the stronger they are. **Spanish onions** are bigger than the bulbs, with a more yellow than brown skin, and most certainly a greater water content. These are the types that are commonly fried and used as a base for stews and soups. While lots of onions have white flesh, the **white onion** has white skin. It is much milder than a standard onion and quite sweet. The **pickling onion** is a little round brown-skinned onion, perfect for pickling.

Pearl onions are very small, white, sweet onions. **Silverskin onions**, also known as 'cocktail' onions, are mainly seen pickled in jars and they are perfect for the job. **Tree onions** grow on trees and have small bulbs on the end of a stubby stem – their flavour is more like garlic than onion.

Part of the draw of a **red onion** is its beautiful colour. Its mild and sweet flavour means it is excellent used raw. In saying that, it is also my favourite variety for roasting whole. A red onion doesn't have the depth of flavour for frying though, and that lovely red tends to become a slushy brown.

Although called an onion, the **Welsh onions** bears little resemblance to the standard bulb type. It's more of a cross between a leek and a chive, and it grows in clusters of six. If you're confused, you will be even more so when I tell you that it has nothing to do with Wales. The Welsh onion is important though, as many varieties of spring onion come from it.

Spring onions were originally the early immature bulb onion, not yet grown or thinned. But as spring onions have become more popular, bulb onions have been developed to mature as a long, thin spring onion, so that we can get them all year round. Clever growers have now developed them whiter and whiter with less and less green. Many successful spring onion varieties come from Welsh onions.

Spring onions are hard to classify. They range from pencil-thin to bigger than a leek, and in many instances begin to resemble a grelot (see below). Generally, the thinner they are, the milder they will be, and fresh ones will sit very happily in your fridge for up to a week. They are of course the perfect vegetable for dipping into things; you get a crunch, a strong allium bite, and a good long handle so you don't get your fingers messy. They will also stir-fry or cook on a griddle pan, but they do cook very quickly. If you chop the green top very finely they are indistinguishable from chives. Red spring onions are now available, but this is all about colour.

The **grelot** is a mature bulbous spring onion. No longer mild or soft enough to be eaten raw (unless sliced very thinly), it is a bunched cooking onion. Because it is so firm, it is not very good for dishes that call for long cooking and onions that will break down. Instead, it is great for quick recipes such as a stir-fry or a frittata.

Cipolline onions are beautiful little flat, turban-shaped sweet onions. Italian in origin, they have a milder flavour making them my favourite accompaniment for balsamic vinegar. Young Massimo at Shambles always gives them to his customers as antipasti with Sardinian music bread (flatbread).

a few facts about onions

Not known as a wild plant, it is difficult to pinpoint exactly where the onion originated. Most scholars believe it must have come from the north of Asia. Mentioned twice in the Bible, onions have been cultivated for around 5,000 years.

Onions were eaten in ancient Egypt from 3,200BC. In Egypt, they were celebrated enough to appear painted on the walls of tombs, and were used as food for slaves and payment to labourers. Yet they were also worshipped by Egyptian priests, who were forbidden to eat them.

Certainly, the onion was a staple of the poor in ancient Egypt, Greece and Rome.

In fact, in all three civilizations, onions were consumed in huge quantities. I like to think of a cheese and onion sandwich as a particularly British invention, but cheese and onions with a drink were always a pleasure for the Greeks and Romans, and the plebeian classes of Rome would have starved without the combination of bread and onions. Better off, more cultivated Romans, looked down on the onion, thinking its smell vulgar and fit only for the poor.

It was the Romans who brought the onion to Britain. We get the name from the Latin '*unio*', meaning 'single white pearl'. From there it went to French as '*oignon*' and then to our 'onion'.

buying onions

Make sure the onion is firm and dry. Onions with brown skins have been left to dry, and it doesn't matter a jot if the skins are peeling off. Look for damp spots; they are a bad thing, and sprouting or green shoots are a sure sign of ageing.

storing onions

When you get onions home, don't put them in the fridge as that smell will get into everything. Keep them in a cool, dark place.

chopping onions and shallots

To finely chop an onion, slice off the top and bottom of the onion 1cm (½ inch) below the hairy or gnarled bit, then peel the onion. Using a sharp knife, halve it from top to base rather than across the middle. Lay the onion half flat-side down on the chopping board and, holding the onion tightly with one hand, cut 3 evenly spaced horizontal slices from side to side, but do not cut all the way through, Next, cut 6 evenly spaced vertical slices (downwards) from top to base, all the way through the three you've already made. Holding the onion together as firmly as you can, cut down 5mm (¼ inch) slices as if slicing into rounds. The onion will now be in little oblongs. Shallots are chopped in the same way, although don't do the horizontal slices for banana shallots.

caramelizing onion slices

Heat 1 tbsp of olive oil and 2 tsp of butter per 200g (7oz) of onions over a medium heat in a pan. Add the onions. Cook over a medium heat until the liquid has evaporated. Lower the heat once the liquid has evaporated and cook the onions for approximately 15–20 minutes in all; the slow-cooking caramelizes the onion, bringing out its sweetness.

deep-frying onions

Slice off the top and bottom of the onion 1cm (½ inch) below the hairy or gnarled bit, then peel the onion. Cut 5mm (¼ inch) whole rounds from each half. Push out the middle bits with your thumb. Dip the rings in milk, then dip them in seasoned flour. Heat a pan of sunflower oil for deep-frying. To test if the oil is hot enough, drop in a little onion – if it sizzles like mad around the onion the temperature is right. Deep-fry the onion in the hot oil for about 2½ minutes, until golden.
Try with: steak.

frying onions and shallots

Onions, gently fried in oil, are the foundation of so many recipes, so it is essential for any cook to be a master of this technique. When used as the base of a dish, onions are more about flavouring than they are about texture – they help to bring together the flavours of other vegetables in a dish. That means you need to chop them very finely (see above). For frying, the first thing to get right is the temperature of the oil: it must be hot – not incredibly hot, just hot – when the onions go in. The fat should sizzle around them when they are added; if it doesn't then the oil's not hot enough. Add the finely chopped onion and cook over a medium heat; once the onions have softened the heat can be increased. If you try to cook them too fiercely or too quickly they will burn, and if they burn you should discard them and the oil they were cooked in.

roasting onions

Preheat the oven to 180°C/350°F/gas mark 4. This is a great cooking method for red or white onions. Peel the onion and trim off the top and tail, cutting away the least amount of onion you can. This will create a flat base. Make a big cross in the top of the onion, cutting half way down through the allium. Put it in the pan next to your roasting joint. As you baste your meat, baste your onion, too. Roast for 30 minutes. If your oven temperature is higher your roasting time will be reduced by a few minutes.
Try with: roasts, in particular roast pork with apples.

soft-frying onion slices

Peel the onion and halve it across the middle. Cut 2.5mm semi-circles from each half. Dip the slices in milk, then dip them in seasoned flour. Heat a frying pan over a medium heat, then add 1 tbsp of olive oil and 2 tsp of butter per 200g (7oz) of onions. When the fat is hot, add the onion slices and cook on a medium heat until soft and brown – roughly 2 minutes.
Try with: steak again.

chargrilling cipolline and grelot onions

Brush the onions with olive oil and cook them over a medium-high heat on a griddle pan, turning all the time, until the outside layer is virtually falling off. The stems of grelot onions are very good chopped into soups or stews.
Try with: harissa.

frying and simmering cipolline and grelot onions

Melt some butter in a frying pan over a medium heat. Add the onions and cook, stirring, for 2 minutes. Cover with water, adding 1 tbsp vinegar and 1 tbsp of sugar per 300g (10½oz) onions. Simmer for a further 10 minutes.

Try with: chargrilled tuna.

roasting cipolline and grelot onions

Brush the onions with olive oil, lay them on a baking tray and roast in the oven at 180°C/350°F/gas mark 4 for 20 minutes.

Try with: roasted Mediterranean veg.

shallots

For many years, I would load lorries at Covent Garden market with vegetables destined for the capital's restaurants, and I never grew tired of throwing a bag of shallots on the truck at the end and shouting to the driver 'that's sha llot'. Writing it now still makes me giggle.

Many people seem unsure when to use a shallot instead of an onion, and who can blame them? I don't believe there is a defining answer to this. I have many cookery books, and some say shallots have a milder flavour than an onion, others that they are stronger, and others that they are sweeter. Some even claim shallots have the strength of an onion without the smell. The argument will never be settled. For a start, which onion is the writer comparing the shallot to? How old or well kept was the shallot? How was it grown? Both an onion and a shallot are powerful alliums and their flavour will differ depending on how they have been grown and stored, without of course considering the many varieties or hybrids there are. I believe that many people recommend shallots because they are more expensive than onions, look prettier and appear more refined.

The major difference between a shallot and an onion is that the onion is one big bulb while the shallot consists of two or more. When a shallot browns in cooking it becomes very bitter, so you should simply soften it in fat. However, the advantage shallots have over onions is their size; if you're cooking for one they are perfect, and of course they can be cooked whole. Onions are more popular than shallots in Europe, but the reverse is true in Asia. The French have popularized shallots over here, adding wine to them to form very good sauces.

I'm often asked what the difference is between a banana and a round shallot. Many people will swear that one tastes different from the other, and I am willing to concede that, on the day they made the comparison, one did taste different from the other, but then two banana shallots brought together from different ends of the country will taste different. Banana shallots, so named because they are long, thin and banana-shaped, I suppose, are the more popular in professional kitchens. This may be because the shape and size fits the aesthetic qualities of any given dish, but I suspect it's about size; if you had to peel and chop 6 kilos of shallots, would you want big or small ones? The banana shallot is easier to peel, too. When peeling smaller ones, put them in boiling water for 3 or 4 minutes and the skin will come off far more easily.

The best-flavoured shallot I've tasted is the **grey skin** shallot. Another good one is the **Jersey** – little, round and bright red, it looks great in my veg basket.

a few facts about shallots

The shallot shares virtually the same history as the onion, but it has many gaps and some believed it to have become extinct. The first written reports are Greek and Roman. What they describe is most certainly a shallot because of the split bulbs, but they both describe it as 'ascolonion'. This shallot is so named because they arrived from the ancient port of Askalon, in what is now Palestine, suggesting that it may have originated from the Middle East.

onion bhajias

This is a bhajia, not a bhaji. My good mate Cyrus Todiwala, of Café Spice Namaste in London, goes bananas when people call the fried sliced onion a bhaji. A bhaji is a vegetable cooked in a sauce. What we have down our curry house on a Saturday night, apart from a load of lager, is a bhajia.

makes 12

125g (4¹/₂ oz) chickpea flour
¹/₂ tsp cayenne
¹/₂ tsp ground coriander
¹/₂ tsp ground cumin
salt and black pepper
2 tbsp chopped coriander
6 tbsp Greek yoghurt
1 large onion, quartered and thinly sliced
vegetable oil

Mix the chickpea flour, spices, salt, pepper, fresh coriander, yoghurt and 80ml (3fl oz) of water together. Mix in the onion.

With your hands, make 12 equal-sized balls with the mixture.

Pour vegetable oil into a wok or big pan to 5cm (2 inches) deep. Heat until it is really hot – a bit of the mixture should sizzle when dropped in.

Gently spoon in the onion balls. Do not move them about. When they are golden below the oil line, turn them and repeat the process on the uncooked side. Allow to drain and cool on kitchen towel. Serve with beer.

lamb chops with onion sauce

This sauce would work very well with chicken or pork, but my preference is for lamb.

serves 4

4 tbsp vegetable oil
2 tbsp sherry vinegar
1 tsp roughly chopped sage
1 clove of garlic, crushed
4 x 200–225g (7–8oz) lamb chump chops
2 medium onions, finely chopped
2 tbsp plain flour
300ml (10fl oz) full-fat milk
1 clove
2 tbsp single cream
¹/₂ tsp freshly grated nutmeg
salt and black pepper

Whisk together the oil, vinegar, sage and garlic. Put the chops in a shallow dish and pour over the marinade. Leave in a cool place, covered, for about an hour.

Remove the chops and place the marinade in a pan with the onions. Cover and cook over a low heat for 15 minutes, until the onions are cooked. Turn up the heat to medium, stir in the flour, then gradually pour in the milk, whisking while you bring it to the boil. When it boils, drop in the clove, reduce the heat, and simmer for 5 minutes. Remove from the heat.

Discard the clove and blitz the sauce with a hand-held blender until smooth. Add the cream and grated nutmeg, and season.

Cook the seasoned chops in a hot griddle pan in their own fat for 6–8 minutes each side. Serve the sauce with the chops.

onion and dill tart

This is what tea time was invented for. If my auntie had baked like this I would have gone to visit her more. Soft sweet onions delivered with a creamy texture in pastry is divine.

serves 6

for the shortcrust pastry

300g (10¹/₂oz) plain flour

150g (5¹/₂oz) cold butter, plus extra for greasing

for the filling

25g (1oz) butter

1 tbsp olive oil

4 onions, finely sliced

¹/₂ tsp freshly grated nutmeg

3 egg yolks, beaten

2 tbsp chopped dill

salt

To make the pastry, sieve the flour into a bowl. Cut the butter (it should be as cold as possible) into small chunks and rub into the flour using your fingertips, until the mixture looks like coarse breadcrumbs. Add 1–2 tbsp of cold water – carefully as you don't want too much – and bring together with your hands. You want a soft but rollable dough. Wrap in clingfilm and chill for an hour.

Preheat the oven to 220°C/425°F/gas mark 7.

Grease a 20cm (8 inch) flan dish. Roll out the pastry and press into the dish. Prick the base. Cut out a circle of greaseproof paper to more than cover all the pastry. Put it over the pastry and fill with dry rice or baking beans. Bake for 10 minutes. Remove the dish and empty out the rice and paper. Return the pastry case to the oven and bake for 5 minutes. Remove from the oven and reduce the heat to 200°C/400°F/gas mark 6.

Meanwhile, for the filling, melt the butter and oil in a pan over a medium heat. Add the onions; you will notice liquid in the bottom of the pan. Whilst you have liquid you can cook on a medium heat. When this evaporates, reduce the heat. Cook for 15–20 minutes, until soft and golden.

Combine the rest of the ingredients in a clean bowl. Add the onions to the mix (not the other way round), then pour the mixture into the pastry case.

Bake for 10 minutes. Reduce the oven temperature to 180°C/350°F/gas mark 4 and cook for another 20 minutes.

poached eggs with onion sauce

This is a really great breakfast. It may not be everyone's cup of tea, but I like it, so I urge you to give it a go.

serves 6

1 onion, thinly sliced into rings
full-fat milk, for soaking
25g (1oz) butter
6 medium slices of white bread
seasoned plain flour, for coating
vegetable oil, for deep-frying
6 eggs

for the sauce

50g (1³/₄oz) butter
225g (8oz) onions, finely chopped
a little plain flour
300ml (10fl oz) full-fat milk
1 tbsp crème fraîche
1 tsp chopped chives
salt and black pepper

Soak the onion rings in the milk for 15 minutes.

For the sauce, melt half the butter in a pan over a medium heat. Add the onions and cook for 15 minutes, until they are very soft. Blitz in a food processor and set aside. Melt the remaining butter in a small pan, add the flour and cook, stirring, for 2 minutes. Gradually pour in the milk, whisking all the time. Add the blitzed onion and simmer for 5 minutes, stirring. Add the crème fraîche, chives and seasoning to taste. Put to one side, covered.

Melt the butter in a frying pan over a medium heat. Add the slices of bread and fry on each side until golden. Remove from the pan and keep warm.

Drain the onion rings, then coat them in seasoned flour. Heat the oil for deep-frying in a heavy-based pan – it is hot enough when a bit of onion sizzles when dropped in. Fry the rings until they are crisp and golden. Keep warm.

Bring a large pan of salted water to the boil. When you have a rolling boil, crack in the eggs and poach 3 at a time for 3–4 minutes, until done to your liking. Meanwhile, reheat the sauce.

Place a piece of fried bread on each plate, top with a poached egg, cover with onion sauce and scatter with onion rings.

bunched onion with harissa and lemon

This is the way I love to eat. It's simple, honest and shows great respect for the alliums. If you lay your hands on good bunched alliums, let them star for a change. They have done their job as a bridging agent many times over. Enjoy them in as natural a state as you can.

serves 4

20 onions with stem, any onion you want

salt

2 tbsp olive oil

4 tbsp harissa

2 lemons, cut into wedges

Cut any dry or rough bits from either end of the onions. Put them in a bowl of boiling salted water for 4 minutes. Drain and dry with kitchen towel.

Heat a griddle pan to hot. Brush the onions with the oil and cook in the pan, turning occasionally, until brown, about 6 minutes, depending on size.

Remove from the heat. Put them in a bowl with the harissa, and completely coat the onions. Serve with the lemon wedges.

roasted red onions with cheese

I love simplicity in food. A red onion is a beautiful thing in its own right, and slowly roasted until soft it's a delight.

serves 4

4 even-sized red onions

a little olive oil, for drizzling

2 tbsp finely chopped parsley

salt and black pepper

100g (3½oz) butter, softened

175g (6oz) Cheshire or Caerphilly cheese, thinly sliced and crumbled

2 tbsp chopped chives

Preheat the oven to 180°C/350°F/gas mark 4. Trim the onions by cutting the papery bit off the top and trimming off the hairy bit.

Put the unpeeled onions in a roasting tin, drizzle on a little olive oil, and cook for 1½ hours, until they feel soft when squeezed.

Meanwhile, mix the parsley and salt and pepper into the softened butter and put aside.

When the onions are cooked, cut a deep cross into each one and open them up. Season and stuff with the herb butter. Scatter the cheese and chives over the onions and serve immediately.

parsnips

I adore parsnips. Roasted and served with any meat, or puréed and served with chicken or beef, they are a delight. Indeed, honey-roasted parsnips must be one of the truly great flavours of a British winter. But my first experience of a parsnip was shocking. My grandmother was a wonderful cook, and to me her roast dinners were the epitome of good food. However, when I was 8 years old she hid a roast parsnip in among my roast potatoes. Thinking it was a potato, I sliced off a big chunk, put it in my mouth and recoiled at its fibrous texture and sweet taste.

I was well into my 20s before I dared venture near a parsnip again, and of course I have now come to appreciate its unusual sweetness.

A lot of the flavour of a parsnip is just under the skin. You must peel them – some of those skins can be really rough – but don't peel them too hard because the flavour is just under the skin. Parsnips are popular in northern Europe, but in southern Europe you hardly ever see them unless you happen to be livestock (in Italy, they are only used as fodder for pigs).

A common mistake when cooking parsnips is to overcook the thin end and undercook the fat bit. You have to equal up the sizes for them to cook evenly. There are classic ways to cook them, but some people like to experiment – today, one of the contestants in the *MasterChef Goes Large* kitchen prepared guinea fowl with a parsnip and blueberry sauce!

Wild parsnips are common in Britain, and are small, woody and inedible. You can find them beside roads, on tracks and next to railway lines. They do especially well in quarries, as they love chalky soil.

types of parsnips

There isn't much to say here, except that you should avoid the baby varieties of parsnips; they have virtually no flavour. If you want small bits of parsnip, just slice them that way.

a few facts about parsnips

In Britain, the parsnip has gone from being a vegetable of huge importance to one with very low esteem. No vegetable has suffered so much from the voyages of Columbus. Before the discovery of sugar, the parsnip's natural sweetness was in high demand, and as a source of starch it was also highly valued. The potato, of course, put a stop to that.

The first parsnips must have been gathered wild and were probably used medicinally or as a flavouring. They may have been used by the ancient Greeks, but in the documentary evidence it is impossible to tell whether they are describing carrots or parsnips. Historians seem more sure that Pliny the Elder – he of the Vesuvius fame –

parsnips

jan	feb	mar	apr	may	jun	jul	aug	sep	oct	nov	dec

described parsnips clearly in the 1st century AD. By the Medieval period, the parsnip had become a huge crop all over northern Europe. The English name 'parsnip' comes from the Latin *'pastinaca'*. The English 'nip' on the end of the word indicated it was similar to a turnip. As well as providing sweetness and starch, medieval physicians credited the humble parsnip with all sorts of health-giving properties.

buying parsnips

Feel the parsnips in your hands; they should be heavy for their size. Make sure the skin isn't split. Avoid huge parsnips as they have an extremely tough stem running through the middle, making them difficult to chop.

storing parsnips

A parsnip will keep in a cool airy place for up to 10 days.

buttering parsnips

Peel and wash the parsnips and cut them into 2cm (¾ inch) chunks – roughly the size of two bits of Yorkie. Bring a pan of salted water to the boil. Add the parsnips and boil for about 10–12 minutes, until tender. Don't stir or boil them too hard as they can break up with rough handling. Drain well. Melt about 25g (1oz) of butter per 100g (3½oz) of parsnips in a frying pan over a medium heat. Add the parsnips and season with lots of salt and pepper. Cook over a medium heat, turning the parsnips often – do not let them brown – for about 2 minutes. In the pan, just before serving, add a soft, green herb of your choice. I use chopped parsley.
Try with: sautéed chicken.

cooking parsnips in cream

Peel and wash the parsnips and cut them into 2cm (¾ inch) chunks. Bring a pan of salted water to the boil. Add the parsnips and boil for about 10–12 minutes, until tender. Drain well. Return the parsnips to the pan and add 4 tbsp of double cream, 1 tbsp of chopped tarragon and some seasoning per 100g (3½oz) of parsnips.
Try with: roast chicken.

deep-frying parsnips

Peel and wash the parsnips and top and tail them. Slice off the thinnest third of each parsnip, then slice the bulbous part into wedges the same size as this third (your

pieces should be no more than 1cm/½ inch wide). Cut away any core that appears hard and woody. Bring a pan of salted water to the boil. Add the parsnips and boil for 10–12 minutes, until tender. Drain well and dry on kitchen towel. Heat some vegetable oil in a heavy bottomed pan. Test that it is hot enough by dropping a slither of parsnip into it – if it sizzles the oil is ready. Add the parsnips, being careful not to overcrowd the pan. Deep-fry for 4 minutes, until golden brown.
Try with: a pork chop.

puréeing parsnips

Peel and wash the parsnips and cut them into 2cm (¾ inch) chunks – roughly the size of 2 bits of Yorkie. Bring a pan of salted water to the boil. Add the parsnips and boil for about 15–20 minutes, until very tender. Don't stir or boil them too hard as they can break up with rough handling. Drain well. Return to the pan and add 4 tbsp of double cream and 25g (1oz) of butter for every 100g (3½oz) of parsnips. Purée using a hand-held blender. Push through a sieve. Season with tons of black pepper.
Try with: roast beef, but add mustard or horseradish, to taste, to the purée first.

roasting parsnips

Peel and wash the parsnips. Slice off the thinnest third of each parsnip, then slice the bulbous part into wedges the same size as this third (your pieces should be no more than 1cm/½ inch wide). Cut away any core that appears hard and woody. Bring a pan of salted water to the boil. Add the parsnips and boil for 5 minutes. Drain well and dry on kitchen towel. Preheat a roasting tray containing vegetable oil to a depth of 1cm (½ inch). Tip the parsnips into the tin and roast for 45 minutes to 1 hour, turning the parsnips every 15 minutes. You want a deep brown colour all over with signs of caramelization.
Try with: roast beef.

Hamburg parsley

A rather bizarre vegetable, the Hamburg parsley – not in any way related to the parsnip, but I had to put it somewhere! I must confess, I knew nothing of this vegetable until a year or so ago, when one of the growers we work with through Secretts Farm suggested that it might be a hit with London chefs. He was right.

Presumably, Hamburg parsley is so-called because of its long parsley-type foliage, but it's actually the small root that is eaten, and this looks like a malnourished parsnip.

It's thinner and squatter than a parsnip and has a smooth velvety texture, with a sweet flavour that is more subtle than a parsnip and a tad nutty. It's easy to prepare and cook; you simply treat it in exactly the same way as you would any other root vegetable. The leaves do taste like parsley, although the herb parsley grows much better and far bigger than the leaf on this root vegetable.

Hamburg parsley has never been popular in Britain but, as its name suggests, it is popular in Germany where, like our parsnip, it is used in soups and stews. It also appears in many Eastern European bortschs. However, we are now taking much more of an interest than we used to in our own home-grown produce and old heirloom varieties, and I think the Hamburg parsley could have a strong future.

cooking Hamburg parsley

Prepare and cook a Hamburg parsley in exactly the same way as you would a parsnip, but don't peel it as it's quite small and slender and you will lose too much of it if you do; you will almost certainly lose most of the flavour.

crispy cheese parsnips

Putting cayenne and Parmesan on a parsnip transforms it completely. I have never matched these with another food; I nibble them in front of the TV.

serves 4

4 medium parsnips

50g (1³/₄oz) Parmesan, finely grated

50g (1³/₄oz) plain flour

1 tsp cayenne pepper

salt and black pepper

dripping, lard or vegetable oil, for roasting

Preheat the oven to 190°C/375°F/gas mark 5.

Cut the parsnips in half lengthways and remove any hard or woody cores.

Bring a large pan of salted water to the boil. Add the parsnips and boil, lid off, for 5 minutes. Drain, but do not allow them to dry out.

In a large plastic food bag, mix together the Parmesan, flour, cayenne, salt and pepper. Add the parsnips and, keeping the bag closed with your hand, shake it well.

In a roasting tin, heat the dripping, lard or vegetable oil over a medium heat. Once it is hot, carefully add the parsnips. Transfer to the oven and roast for 30–40 minutes, turning parsnips over once half-way through cooking.

curried parsnip soup

I know, I know, parsnip soup is a Jane Grigson classic! It is lovely, though. Go for a long walk in the winter without proper winter clothing. Get really cold, just so you can warm yourself back up again with this soup. It can be kept in the fridge for a few days and reheated when you fancy it.

serves 4

25g (1oz) butter

2 tbsp sunflower oil

1 onion, thinly sliced

500g (1lb 2oz) parsnips, diced

1 potato, cut into medium dice

3 tbsp medium curry powder

1.2 litres (2 pints) chicken stock

1 clove of garlic, crushed

salt and black pepper

4 tbsp double cream, to serve

Melt the butter with the oil in a large pan over a low heat. Add the onion, parsnips and potato and sweat, lid on, for about 15 minutes. Stir regularly; do not allow the vegetables to brown.

Add the curry powder and cook, stirring, for 10 minutes. Add the stock and garlic. Remove the lid from the pan, increase the heat, and simmer for about 20 minutes, until the vegetables can be easily pierced with a fork.

Blitz the soup with a hand-held blender, then put it through a sieve. Season to taste. Serve in bowls with a swirl of cream on top.

peas

I am a big fan of peas. Maybe it's my love of mint (I do love peas cooked with a spoonful of sugar and a large sprig of mint), maybe it's my sweet tooth, or maybe it's my lazy streak and the fact that you don't have to chew them. I once had a Slovakian friend, Yana, who thought the English custom of trying to balance little green balls on the back of a curved fork was ridiculous. I feel she missed the point – I squash my peas into whatever fish, meat or potato is going on the fork with them, sweetening the whole lot wonderfully.

To properly enjoy fresh peas you must grow them. If you don't, then stroll down to the local allotment and make friends with someone who does. All vegetables deteriorate once they have been picked, but nothing deteriorates as quickly as a pea. Frozen peas can be good; in fact most peas now are bred with freezing in mind. And canned peas can be nice too; I love processed peas – the processing exaggerates their sweetness.

types of peas

The most popular variety of pea in Britain is the **garden pea**. The **petit pois** was originally a garden pea harvested very early. However, things have changed and now some petit pois are dwarf varieties of pea that mature stunted.

When I started working at Secrett's Farm I invested a huge amount of time in thumbing through seed catalogues looking for the **marrowfat pea**. Finally I realised that it isn't a variety at all, it's just a big pea treated with alkali to make it mushy.

The **sugar-snap** pea and the **mange-tout** were both once just immature pea pods, where the pea inside had barely formed. These days, although closely related to the pea, they are different varieties. The mange-tout is flat, with an almost rubbery texture and a spine running down one side; I would avoid it. The sugar-snap is a round, more tubular affair, which is beautifully sweet even when eaten raw, and which gives a little crunch. If the pea has formed a string down one side I would pull it off. They soften with the lightest of steaming and do very well tossed in a pan with melted butter. Garden pea pods are inedible (although not if picked when they are babies).

a few facts about peas

The pea may be synonymous with Western cuisine, but it originated in Western Asia. Dried pea seeds, dating back to 5,700BC, have been found in excavations of Jericho. The discovery of Troy came with the excavation of what must be the biggest jar of peas ever, weighing in at a colossal 220kg (495lb). That, my friends, is a lot of peas.

We know garden peas were eaten in Bronze Age settlements in Switzerland in 3000BC. They were grown by the Greeks and Romans, and they spread from the Roman Empire into India and then to China by the 7th century. In those days most peas would have been dried, and it's nice to think that it was probably the grower and his family that got to eat the fresh ones rather than the lofty lord he grew them for.

| jan | feb | mar | apr | may | jun | jul | aug | sep | oct | nov | dec |

buying peas

If you can, pop a pod to check the peas are round and full but still soft. Otherwise, check the outside of the pods are bright green and have a sort of satiny look.

storing peas

You can store peas, but you will miss the whole point. Hunt down fresh ones!

boiling peas

The older the pea, the more cooking it will need. Shell the peas. Bring a large pan of unsalted water to the boil. Add the peas, plus a few mint leaves and 1 tbsp of sugar for every 100g (3½oz) of peas and cook for 2–4 minutes until soft. Drain. Remove the mint.
Try with: fish fingers, boiled potatoes and butter.

puréeing peas

Bring a large pan of unsalted water to the boil. Add the peas, plus a few mint leaves and 1 tbsp sugar for every 100g (3½oz) peas, and cook for 3–6 minutes, depending on the age of the pea, until soft. Drain. Put in a processor with 300ml (10fl oz) of single cream, crème fraîche or the peas' cooking liquid for every 100g (3½oz) of peas, and purée.
Try with: lamb chops.

steaming peas and mange-tout

Put the peas in a pan with, for every 100g (3½oz) of peas, 2 tbsp of veg stock, 15g (½oz) of butter and a sprig of mint. Steam, lid on, on a medium heat for 5 minutes (2½ for mangetout). Do not lift the lid to look. Remove the mint and strain off any liquid.
Try with: fish.

boiling mange-tout

Bring a large pan of unsalted water to the boil. Add the mange-tout and cook for 1 minute. Drain immediately and instantly rinse under the cold tap.
Try with: lamb and mashed potato.

stir-frying mange-tout

Heat 1 tbsp vegetable oil and 1 tsp sesame oil in a wok on a high heat. Add the mange-tout and stir-fry for 1 minute.
Try with: a green salad.

minted pea purée with lamb chops

Boy, I love lamb. My earliest memory of an outstanding meal is my late and dearly loved grandmother's roast lamb, served with mint sauce, made from mint cut from pots in her garden. Since then the combination of mint and lamb has stayed with me as possibly my favourite flavour combination in the world. It can be no coincidence that my brother Biffo holds those flavours close to his heart, too.

serves 4

4 tsp caster sugar

500g (1lb 2oz) peas, podded

2 tbsp sunflower oil

8 lamb chops

1/2 bunch of mint leaves

6 tbsp double cream

8 tbsp white wine vinegar

boiled potatoes, to serve

Bring a pan of unsalted water to the boil. Add half the sugar and the peas, and cook until soft, about 4 minutes. Drain.

Heat the oil in a pan over a medium heat. Add the chops. Cook for 6–8 minutes on each side, depending on size and how you like them.

Meanwhile, put the peas in a clean pan and blitz with a hand-held blender. Add the mint and blitz again. Put the pea pan on a low heat and stir in the cream. Stir in the rest of the sugar and the vinegar.

Serve the pea purée with the chops and some boiled potatoes.

minted pea soup

This is a very simple and very delicious recipe.

serves 4–6

25g (1oz) butter

1 onion, finely chopped

375g (13oz) lettuce leaves, chopped

1 tbsp plain flour

500g (1lb 2oz) peas, podded

1.2 litres (2 pints) vegetable or chicken stock

1 tsp caster sugar

2 large mint sprigs

salt and black pepper

3 tbsp crème fraîche

Melt the butter in a large pan over a medium heat. Add the onion and cook gently until soft. Add the lettuce and cook for a couple of minutes, stirring. Stir in the flour and cook for a further 2 minutes.

Add the peas, stock, sugar and mint, then bring to the boil, cover and simmer for about 20 minutes, until soft. Remove the mint and discard.

Transfer the soup to a food processor and purée until smooth. Rinse out the pan. Return the smooth soup to the pan, reheat, check the seasoning and stir in the crème fraîche.

pea risotto

When this is ready, your guests must be ready to eat – a lukewarm risotto is not good!

serves 4–6

60g (2¹/₄oz) butter

1 tbsp olive oil

2 rashers streaky bacon, finely chopped

2 shallots, finely chopped

1.2 litres (2 pints) vegetable or chicken stock

250g (9oz) peas, podded

165g (5³/₄oz) risotto rice

1 tbsp chopped parsley

salt and black pepper

Parmesan, grated, to serve

Melt half the butter with the oil in a large pan over a medium heat. Add the bacon and shallots and cook for about 5 minutes, until soft.

Place the stock in a small pan and keep it warm over a very low heat. Add half the peas to the stock.

Add the rice and the rest of the peas to the bacon and shallots and cook, stirring, for 2 minutes. Add the stock to the rice a ladleful at a time; stir in the stock, and do not add any more until the last lot has evaporated. Keep stirring all the time.

When the rice is almost cooked and there is only 1–2 ladlefuls of stock left, blitz the remaining pea and stock mixture together with a hand-held blender, then continue using the stock – the risotto is cooked when the rice is tender but retains a little bite. Season.

Stir in the rest of the butter and the parsley. Serve immediately with a bowl of grated Parmesan separately for your guests to sprinkle on themselves.

French peas

You don't normally think of cooking a lettuce, but the gem is a hardy fellow. Peas and onions sticking on to gem by means of salty butter fills my heart with joy.

serves 4

500g (1lb 2oz) peas, podded

2 baby gem lettuces, halved

12 small pickling onions, peeled

60g (2¹/₄oz) butter

2 sprigs parsley

2 sprigs chervil

1 tsp caster sugar

salt and black pepper

Put all the ingredients apart from the salt and pepper in a large pan with 4 tbsp of water. Cover and cook over a low heat for 15–20 minutes, until the peas are tender, shaking the pan occasionally.

Check the seasoning. Remove the herbs before serving.

fish and pea terrine

This is right up there with my favourite recipes of all time. The first time I made it I was so pleased with myself! As I turned the dish upside down and the terrine dropped gently on to the plate, in one piece, I literally danced a little jig of joy!

serves 8

1 tbsp vegetable oil, for greasing

450g (1lb) salmon fillet, skinned

450g (1lb) sole fillet, skinned

salt and black pepper

3 egg whites

100ml (3½fl oz) double cream

2 tbsp finely chopped chives

a few gratings of nutmeg

juice of 1 lemon

115g (4oz) peas, podded and cooked

1 tsp chopped mint

Preheat the oven to 200°C/400°F/gas mark 6. Grease a 1 litre (2lb) terrine or loaf tin with the vegetable oil. Cut the salmon and sole into long strips, 2.5cm (1 inch) wide.

Line the terrine neatly with alternate slices of salmon and sole, leaving the ends hanging over the edge, reserving about a third of salmon and a third of sole.

Purée the remaining sole in a food processor, then put it in a bowl and season. In a large bowl, beat the egg whites with a pinch of salt until they form soft peaks. Fold two-thirds of the egg whites into the processed sole, followed by two-thirds of the cream and some seasoning. Put half the mixture into a second bowl and stir the chives into this bowl. Season the first bowl with nutmeg.

Purée the remaining salmon and put it in a third bowl. Add the lemon and fold in the remaining egg whites and cream. Season.

Purée the peas with the mint and season. Spread the peas over the base of the terrine, smoothing with a spatula. Spoon over the sole and chive mixture and smooth it with a spatula. Add the salmon mixture, again smoothing with the spatula, then finish with the plain sole mixture, which also needs smoothing. Cover with the overhanging pieces of fish.

Make a lid of oiled kitchen foil and place on top of the terrine. Stand the terrine in a roasting tin and pour in enough boiling water from the kettle to come halfway up the sides.

Carefully place in the oven and bake for 15–20 minutes, until the top fillets are just cooked. Remove the foil, lay a wire rack over the top of the terrine and invert both on to a lipped dish to catch the cooking juices that leak out.

Leave the terrine to stand for about 15 minutes, then turn it over again, invert it on to a serving dish. Serve warm or chilled from the fridge.

spring veg and lamb stew

Lamb and veg is a greengrocer's dream combination!

serves 4–6

60g (2¼oz) butter

1 tbsp vegetable oil

1.5kg (3lb 5oz) boned shoulder
of lamb, cubed

2 onions, finely sliced

2 tbsp plain flour

450g (1lb) potatoes, roughly
chopped

225g (8oz) tomatoes, skinned
and chopped

1 x bouquet garni

salt and black pepper

1 litre (1¾ pints) lamb, chicken
or vegetable stock

225g (8oz) small turnips, peeled
and quartered

350g (12oz) baby carrots, sliced

675g (1lb 8oz) very small new
potatoes

450g (1lb) peas, podded

Preheat the oven to 170°C/325°F/gas mark 3.

Melt the butter and oil in large ovenproof pot over a medium heat. Add the cubes of lamb – don't crowd the pot, do this in batches. Once they are brown all over, remove from the pot and keep to one side while you fry the rest. Remove all the lamb from the pot.

Add the onions to the pot and cook until they are slightly brown. Stir in the flour and cook, stirring, for a couple of minutes.

Return the meat to the pot and add the potatoes, tomatoes, bouquet garni, salt and pepper to taste, and stock. Bring to the boil, cover, and place in the oven for 1 hour.

Remove the pot from the oven. Uncover, and mash the potatoes as much as you can. Add the turnips and carrots, cover, and return to the oven for another hour.

Towards the end of the cooking time, bring a large pan of salted water to the boil. Add the new potatoes and parboil fo 5 minutes. Drain.

When the lamb has been cooking for 2 hours, add the cooked new potatoes and the peas to the lamb and return to the oven for a further 20 minutes. Check the seasoning before serving.

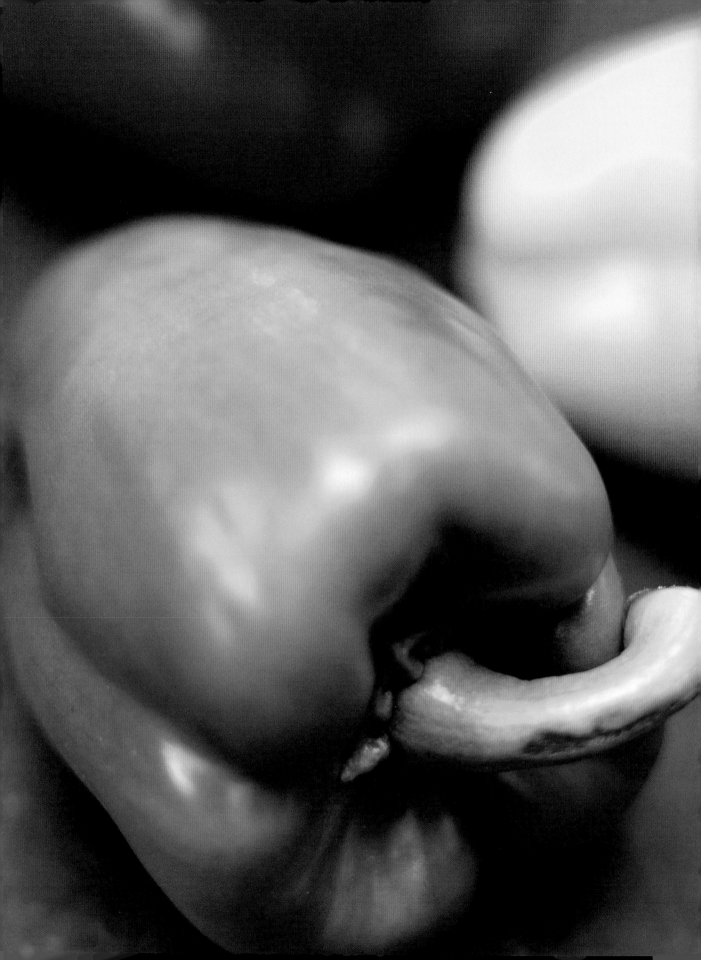

peppers

Although the pepper originated in the New World, it is now seen very much as a Mediterranean vegetable. I really dislike peppers, and I think it's because I've eaten so many bland ones. I mean, have you ever grown any veg? If you have you'll realise how difficult it is to get any two veg to grow to exactly the same shape and size. So when you see a supermarket shelf stocked with hundreds of peppers, all exactly the same weight and size, trust your instincts; something has gone badly wrong.

types of pepper

The peppers we usually see are **bell peppers**. They are a capsicum, from the same family as chillies. There are flavoursome peppers, but supermarkets don't tend to stock them, presumably because they are as ununiform as ununiform can be. If you put lots of these beauties together, some will be flat, some bulbous, and some a mixture of the two; some will be the same colour all over and some will look like paint's been spilt on them. She's an awkward cuss that Mother Nature; she simply refuses to be bar-coded.

At their best, peppers are large, fleshy and mildly chilli-flavoured. The **green** ones are bitter, the **red** ones are sweet, and the **yellow** ones are a lighter-tasting version of the two mixed together. Orange ones are just silly; I've no idea where they originated. All red ones were once green, but not all green ones will go red. A strain of green has been developed that will stay green when ripened. Oh yippidy doo.

China is Asia's biggest grower of peppers and Spain is Europe's. There's little to distinguish between the Spanish and Dutch peppers; most just taste bland.

a few facts about peppers

Originally from Central America, pepper seeds were carried by birds and spread over all but the harshest environments of the American Continent.

buying and storing peppers

Buy peppers that can rot; a box of peppers should be unevenly shaped and coloured. Most of the peppers you buy won't rot; they just grow funny white beards up the side.

blanching peppers

Blanching peppers before stuffing gives them a more delicate flavour. Remove the core, stem, internal membranes and seeds, keeping the peppers whole. Bring a pan of salted water to the boil. Boil the peppers for 1–2 minutes, pushing them under the water. Drain.

grilling and skinning peppers

Cut peppers into quarters and remove the stem, internal membranes and seeds. Place the quarters, skin-side up, under a hot grill. Grill until blackened and blistered all over. Place in a bowl and cover with clingfilm. When cool enough, peel off the skins.

jan	feb	mar	apr	may	jun	jul	aug	sep	oct	nov	dec

grilled vegetable terrine

I know there's a lot of prep involved here, but the results are spectacular. This dish is just as deep in colour as it is in flavour.

serves 6

2 large red peppers, quartered, cored and deseeded

2 large yellow peppers, quartered, cored and deseeded

1 large aubergine, sliced lengthways

6 tbsp olive oil

2 large courgettes, sliced lengthways

vegetable oil, for greasing

400ml (14fl oz) tomato juice

2 tbsp powdered gelatine

bunch of basil

salt and black pepper

for the dressing

6 tbsp extra virgin olive oil

2 tbsp sherry vinegar

Cook the prepared peppers, skin-side up, under a hot grill until the skins have blackened. Transfer to a bowl, cover with clingfilm and leave to cool. Peel.

Heat a griddle pan. Brush one side of the aubergine slices with olive oil and put them in the hot pan, oiled-side down. While cooking, brush the upper sides with oil. Cook on both sides until brown and soft.

Do the same with the courgette slices.

Lightly brush a 1.75 litre (3 pint) terrine dish with vegetable oil, then line it with clingfilm, leaving a little hanging over the edges.

Pour half the tomato juice into a pan, sprinkle on the gelatine and dissolve over a very low heat, stirring to prevent lumps.

Place a layer of red peppers in the base of terrine, then pour in enough of the tomato juice to cover.

Continue layering the aubergine, courgettes and peppers, pouring gelatine juice over each layer and adding a couple of basil leaves on each layer. Season with salt and pepper. Finish with a layer of red peppers.

Add the remaining tomato juice to the juice left in the pan and pour this over the terrine. Give the terrine a sharp tap to settle the juices. Cover and chill until set.

To make the dressing, whisk together the olive oil and vinegar with some salt and pepper. When the terrine is set and chilled, turn it out of the dish carefully and peel off the cling film. Serve in thick slices with the dressing poured over.

tomato and green pepper goulash

What is it about beef and tomatoes? I have loved this combination since I was a child. I have experimented (mostly unsuccessfully, I must admit) with these 2 ingredients for years. This goulash recipe is by far the best beef and tomato combo I have made.

serves 4–6

4 tbsp vegetable oil

900g (2lb) stewing steak, cubed

1 onion, finely chopped

2 cloves of garlic, crushed

3 green peppers, cored, deseeded and diced

2 tbsp paprika

1kg (2lb 4oz) tomatoes, skinned and chopped

1 tbsp chopped parsley

1 tbsp chopped oregano

2 tsp granulated sugar

salt and black pepper

Heat the oil in a large pan over a medium heat. Fry the meat in small batches until it is brown all over. Transfer the meat to a dish and leave it to one side.

In the same frying pan, fry the onion and garlic for 3 minutes. Add the peppers and paprika. Cook, stirring, for 1 minute.

Return the meat to the pan and add the tomatoes, herbs and sugar. Season well, then bring to the boil, cover and simmer for 1½ hours, until the meat is tender. Serve with freshly boiled rice.

potato

The potato is my favourite vegetable. Can you imagine where we would be without it? For a start, is there anyone alive who doesn't love a chip – that hot, portable food, so crispy on the outside and soft in the middle? One of my great indulgences is to cook far more new potatoes than I could possibly manage for dinner, leave them in the fridge overnight, then slice them and fry them in butter the next morning. These crispy little beauties, dipped into a peppered fried egg, are sublime. And what about roast potatoes? Hang on a minute – what about mash, the ultimate comfort food?

There's English mash, which you spoon out of a bowl, and French mash, which you pour. When you're feeling sad, mash is good; when you're feeling happy, mash is good; on a rainy day, mash is good. I believe, with a perfect plate of food, you should be mopping up the last bit of wet with the last bit of dry, and this is why mash is so clever – it mops up and is both wet and dry at the same time.

The potato is a tuber (a swollen root). Not only is it the world's most versatile vegetable, it is also the third biggest food crop, pipped to the post by maize and rice. From humble beginnings as a New World crop that was virtually forced on to the poor of Europe, it is now a staple for two-thirds of the world's population. A field of potatoes throws up more food per acre than any other European food crop. Potatoes grow well in all but the harshest of environments and they are packed with vitamin C.

Although the potato is a huge success in Europe, a survey from 1998 has China as the biggest grower, growing an estimated 41 million tonnes a year. How would we feed ourselves without our friendly spud? And do you know why we call them 'spuds'? A spud was the original three-pronged fork used by the Irish to dig potatoes.

types of potato

Potatoes do different jobs. To me, the major difference is between varieties suited to mashing or chipping. Chippers need to be starchy, mashers fluffy. Don't think you can buy one potato that will do every job. To add to the confusion, all potatoes are held in storage. If you find a variety that chips well, the chances are that the longer it's been held in storage, the more of its starch will have turned to sugar, and this is when you get that awful caramelization of chips in the pan. Even more confusing is the fact that the same variety may be grown on different farms, even if it's packed in one place and sold under one brand, making each bag of potatoes slightly different from the next. My advice to any chip-lover is to regularly change the variety you use during the year.

You'll often see the words 'floury' and 'waxy' on a bag of spuds. New potatoes are waxy, which means they don't absorb much liquid. Waxy potatoes are good for boiling, while you want floury ones for both mashing and chipping.

One misconception is the difference between a new and a salad potato. All new potatoes are salad potatoes, but not all salad potatoes are new. A salad potato is just

| jan | feb | mar | apr | may | jun | jul | aug | sep | oct | nov | dec |

a small, waxy potato; you can only call it new if it has been just dug; if you can rub the skin off with your thumb, it's new; if not, it's a salad potato.

Here's a checklist of which common varieties best suit which dishes. Follow this and you'll be in spud heaven for the rest of your days:

New potatoes: **Jersey.**

Salad potatoes: **Belle de Fontenay, Ratte, Pink Fir Apple, Charlotte.**

Boiled potatoes: **Bintje, Cyprus, any newly dug Estima.**

Baked potatoes: **Aaron, King Edward, all of the boilers.**

Roast potatoes: **Cara, Desirée.**

Chips: **Bintje, Cyprus, Kipfler, Arran Pilot, Ausonia, Spunta, Home Guard, Maris Bard.**

Mash: **Golden Wonder, Wilja, Pentland Dell, Marfona.**

All rounders: **Maris Piper, King Edward, Cara, Romano.**

a few facts about potatoes

Historians believe that the potato was being cultivated in the area we now know as Peru around 2,000 years ago – some say as early as 3,000BC! Just pause for a moment and consider that. Before that, allegedly, South Americans were eating it and worshipping it between 7,000 and 10,000BC. Now, I know there are some clever historians, but how can anyone tell someone prayed to a potato 12,000 years ago?

The European discovery of the potato happened in 1537 by Spanish explorer Jimenez de Quesada. The potato in Europe has a rich history. The same stories are repeated over and over: one of the landed gentry trying to convince the poor to accept potatoes as a means of warding off starvation; the other of the common yeomanry of Europe refusing to have anything to do with a food closely related to the poisonous deadly nightshade. Protestant Europe took even longer to accept the potato. In fact, one English 18th century election slogan ran 'no potatoes, no popery'. The difficulty in convincing a hungry population to accept the potato should not be underestimated. It amazes me that of two crops brought back from the New World, potatoes took twice as long to establish as Jerusalem artichokes.

There is one example of this struggle that I would like to relate – the Frenchman Antoine Auguste Parmentier managed to convince King Louis XVI of the potato's future, but couldn't do the same with the poor of Paris. The method he employed was brilliant in its simplicity. He planted potatoes on common ground on the outskirts of the great city, then convinced the King to lend him some armed guards, who he posted at intervals around the edge of field. Thinking the guards were guarding something of great value, the urban poor crept in every night and stole the lot. It worked a treat! Parmentier's next bold move was to convince Marie Antoinette to wear potato flowers in her hair. The potato was unknown in North America when it first hit the shores of Europe. It came from Central and South America to Europe and then sailed back across the Atlantic with the Pilgrim Fathers in 1621.

Ireland's love of the potato is well documented, although how the spud got to the country is unclear. There are two schools of thought: one is that Sir Walter Raleigh brought potatoes back from the Americas and planted them on his estate in Ireland; the other is that they were washed up from the wreck of the Armada.

buying potatoes

Try to buy potatoes with plenty of dirt on. The earth around them acts as a protective layer; they don't like sunlight or heat. Keep them in a cool, dark place. The best way to buy them is straight from the farms or along the roadside. If you've got a family big enough, and a kitchen big enough, to cope with a 25kg sack, you will get a bargain.

storing potatoes

If you buy potatoes from a supermarket, get them out of that silly plastic bag as soon as possible, as condensation will form inside it and start to rot your spuds. If you are going to store them for a while, squeeze them from time to time to make sure they are firm and check they are not sprouting. When storing potatoes, remember that green is bad; it's poison. It may not do you any harm, but it could, and with your average potato costing less than a bootlace, is it really worth the risk? Just throw them out.

baking potatoes

Preheat the oven to 220°C/425°F/gas mark 7. Scrub the potatoes under running water with a brush. Stab them with a fork 2–3 times. Bake on an oven shelf for 1 hour. Squeeze the potato using a tea towel to test if it's cooked, cut a cross in it and squeeze to open. Try with: butter.

boiling salad potatoes

Wash the potatoes. Bring a pan of salted water to the boil. Add the potatoes and boil, lid on, for 15 minutes. You could add a sprig of mint to the water with the potatoes. Try with: melted butter.

boiling old potatoes

Peel waxy potatoes and cut them into pieces no bigger than an egg. Bring a pan of salted water to the boil. Add the potatoes and boil, lid on, for about 20 minutes, until tender. Try with: melted butter and finely chopped parsley.

making chips

You need large floury, starchy potatoes that are even in size. Peel the spuds and cut them into uniform chips. Soak in cold water for 30 minutes, then drain and dry with kitchen towel. Place enough oil in a deep, heavy pan to come no more than halfway up the pan's sides. Heat over a gentle heat to 140°C/275°F, or until a cube of bread put in the oil turns brown in less than 1 minute. Gently lower the potatoes into the oil and cook until soft (not brown); 5 minutes. Lift out the chips. Increase the temperature of the oil to 190°C/375°F, or until a bread cube turns brown in 30 seconds. Lower the chips in again and fry until brown and crisp. Drain on kitchen towel and season. Try with: fish in batter.

mashing potatoes

Peel floury, fluffy potatoes and cut them into pieces no bigger than an egg. Bring a pan of salted water to the boil. Add the potatoes and boil, lid on, for 15–20 minutes, until very tender. Drain in a colander. Return the potatoes to the pan and place over a gentle heat, shaking it all the time, for 2 minutes to dry the spuds. In another small pan, put 55g (2oz) of butter and 30ml (1fl oz) of milk (or cream or crème fraîche) per 1kg (2lb 4oz) potatoes until the butter has melted and the milk is hot. Mash the potatoes dry. Add the milk and butter to the potatoes and beat. Add milk until it's how you like it. Try with: pork chops.

roasting potatoes

Preheat the oven to 200°C/400°F/gas mark 6. Peel floury starchy potatoes and cut them into convenient sized pieces. Bring a pan of salted water to the boil. Add the potatoes and boil, lid on, for 5 minutes. Drain well in a colander. Return the potatoes to the pan, put the lid on and shake vigorously; they should look like they have been floured. Preheat some dripping, lard or vegetable oil in a roasting tray, then add the potatoes. Roast for about 50 minutes, or with your joint for longer if the temperature is lower, turning the potatoes over every 15 minutes. Drain on kitchen towel and season with salt. Try with: roast meats.

patatas bravas

The combination of fried small potatoes and tomatoes with a hint of chilli is very fine.
I have always held to the wet and dry theory of food. The last bit of dry food on
your plate should be mopping up the last bit of wet. This dish proves my theory.

serves 4

6 tbsp olive oil

1kg (2lb 4oz) cooked salad
potatoes, cooled and halved

1 onion, finely chopped

2 cloves of garlic, crushed

1 tbsp tomato purée

227g tin chopped tomatoes

1 tbsp red wine vinegar

4 red chillies, deseeded and
finely chopped (if you want
more heat, chuck in the seeds)

1 tsp paprika

salt and black pepper

parsley leaves, to garnish

Heat 2 tbsp of the oil in a very large frying pan. Add the potatoes
and cook, stirring regularly, for about 15 minutes, until golden
brown and crispy.

Meanwhile, heat the remaining oil in a pan over a low to medium
heat. Add the onion and garlic and cook gently for 6 minutes

Add all the other ingredients, apart from the parsley, to the onion.
Cover, and gently cook for 5 minutes.

Combine the sauce with the potatoes, give it a good stir and cook
for another 5 minutes. Serve up sprinkled with parsley.

new potato, watercress and bacon salad

There is no need to reinvent the wheel. Crisp bacon, hot watercress and soft potato are
a brilliant combination.

serves 4

salt and black pepper

700g (1lb 9oz) small, waxy new
potatoes such as Jersey,
scrubbed

8 rashers streaky bacon

140ml (4½fl oz) soured cream

1 tbsp olive oil

1 tbsp chopped chives

2 tbsp sherry vinegar

medium bunch of watercress

Bring a pan of salted water to the boil. Drop in the potatoes and
boil for about 15 minutes, until cooked. Drain in a colander, cool
under a cold tap and set aside to cool completely.

Grill the bacon under a medium heat until crisp. Cut up into
pieces the size you like and set aside.

In a small jug, mix the soured cream, olive oil, chives and vinegar.
Season to taste.

Wash the watercress and remove the tough stalks.

When the potatoes are cool, put them in a bowl. Add the chopped
bacon, dressing and watercress and mix well.

salad potatoes roasted with fennel and garlic

This is an unusual take on salad potatoes. The anise flavour of the fennel, the spicy kick of the paprika and the softness of the salad potatoes make this dish an irresistible treat for a summer's evening.

serves 4–6

15 saffron threads

salt and black pepper

500g (1lb 2oz) salad potatoes, washed and cut into wedges

1 bulb of garlic, unpeeled and separated into cloves

12 baby onions or shallots, peeled

2 bulbs of fennel, cut into wedges

4 bay leaves

6 sprigs of thyme

175ml (6fl oz) vegetable stock

2 tbsp sherry vinegar

1 tsp granulated sugar

1 tbsp fennel seeds, lightly crushed

1 tsp paprika

1 tbsp chopped dill

3 tbsp olive oil

Soak the saffron in 2 tbsp of warm water for at least 10 minutes. Preheat the oven to 190°C/375°F/gas mark 5.

Bring a pan of salted water to the boil. Drop in the potatoes and boil, lid on, for 5–10 minutes.

Peel and finely chop 2 cloves of garlic and set aside.

Drain the potatoes and put them in a large roasting tin with the unpeeled garlic cloves, the onions or shallots, the fennel, bay leaves and thyme.

In a jug, mix the stock and saffron water together. Add the vinegar, sugar, fennel seeds, paprika, dill, chopped garlic and olive oil and mix well. Pour over the vegetables.

Cover the roasting tin and roast the veg for about 1 hour, stirring occasionally. The vegetables should be tender; if not, cook for a further 15 minutes.

roast salad potatoes with caviar and soured cream

Feeling rich? This is pure decadence. My advice is serve this with a big glass of water and a smaller glass of chilled vodka.

serves 4

1kg (2lb 4oz) salad potatoes (try to get them all the same size)

1 tbsp olive oil

salt and black pepper

100ml (3½fl oz) soured cream

100g (3½oz) caviar (whichever suits your pocket)

1 tbsp finely chopped chives, to serve

Preheat the oven to 200°C/400°F/gas mark 6. Bring a large pan of salted water to the boil. Add the potatoes and boil for 10–15 minutes. Drain in a colander.

Put the oil in a roasting tin and place over a medium heat. When it is hot, roll the potatoes in it, season, then roast for 30 minutes.

While hot, cut a cross in the potatoes and squeeze gently from the bottom. The effect will be 4 raised spud quarters in each potato with a crevice in between.

Spoon on equal amounts of cream and caviar. Sprinkle with the chives to serve.

champ

One of the many great things to come from Ireland is champ. It's one of the most comforting things to eat that I know.

serves 4

750g (1lb 10oz) good mashing potatoes

6 spring onions, green part trimmed and removed, white part sliced

300ml (10fl oz) full-fat milk

salt and black pepper

tons of butter, to taste

Peel the potatoes and cut them into equal sizes so they will all cook in the same time.

Put the spring onion slices in a pan with the milk. Bring to the boil and simmer, lid on, for 15-20 minutes.

Meanwhile, bring a large pan of salted water to the boil. Add the potatoes and boil for 20 minutes. They are ready when a knife goes through the potato without resistance. Immediately drain well and return to the pan.

Mash the potatoes with a masher – mash as little as possible, or your potatoes will taste like wallpaper paste. Add the milk and onion mixture as you go. Season well.

Put the champ on serving plates and make a indentation in the top of each mound. Put a knob of butter in each hollow.

Spanish omelette

This is a proper Spanish omelette. You will notice it does not contain peppers, anchovies or ham. My main problem with this dish is allowing the thing to cool. My kids and I tend to munch the living daylights out of it straight from the pan. Turning the omelette from the pan to a plate and back again is pure kitchen theatre.

serves 4–6

3 tbsp olive oil

2 large onions, finely sliced

1kg (2lb 4oz) baking potatoes (King Edwards or Maris Piper)

8 eggs, gently beaten

salt and black pepper

Preheat the oven to 190°C/375°F/gas mark 5.

Heat 2 tbsp olive oil in a frying pan over a low heat. Add the onions. Cook for 15–20 minutes, until soft and golden.

Peel and chop the potatoes into 1cm (½ inch) dice. Rinse and drain in a colander. Put the potatoes in an ovenproof dish, cover, and bake for 10–15 minutes, until they are soft.

Put the eggs in a bowl and add the cooked onions and potatoes. Season to taste.

Heat the remaining oil in a frying pan over a medium heat. Add the omelette mixture and flatten it all out. Cook for about 20 minutes; the omelette must be firm on the base but a little runny on the top.

Remove the pan from the heat and place a large plate over it – the plate must completely cover the pan. Turn everything upside down so the omelette is on the plate. Slide the omelette back into the pan, uncooked-side down, and cook for a further 6 minutes.

Jansson's temptation

This is obviously a Scandinavian dish. It does take quite a while to cook, but anchovies slowly melting into potato is a dream!

serves 4

50g (1³/₄oz) butter

900g (2lb) large potatoes, peeled

salt and black pepper

2 large onions, thinly sliced

2 x 50g tins anchovies in olive oil, drained

500ml (18fl oz) whipping cream

Preheat the oven to 200°C/400°F/gas mark 6. Grease a gratin dish with 15g (½oz) butter.

Using a sharp knife, slice the potatoes thinly, then cut them into fine matchsticks. Toss them with salt and pepper and place half of them in the bottom of the gratin dish.

Lay half the onions on top of the potatoes and season, then lay the anchovies on top, then add the rest of the onions and season again. Finally top with the rest of the potatoes.

Mix the cream with 2 tbsp of cold water and pour over the potatoes. If necessary, add a little cold milk to bring the liquid to just below the top of the final layer of potatoes.

Dot the potatoes with the remaining butter, cover with foil and bake for 1 hour.

Reduce the heat to 180°C/350°F/gas mark 4 and remove the foil. Bake for a further 40–50 minutes, until the potatoes are tender and brown.

mini fish and sweetcorn pies

These handy mini fish pies are richly satisfying. Great comfort food for grown-ups and kids alike!

serves 6

6 large even-sized baking potatoes such as King Edward, scrubbed

4 sweetcorn cobs

60g (2¼oz) butter, plus extra melted butter, for drizzling

150g (5½oz) smoked haddock, cooked, cooled and flaked

1 tbsp chopped chives

salt and black pepper

30ml (1fl oz) full-fat milk

12 tbsp crème fraîche

25g (1oz) Cheddar, grated

Preheat the oven to 200°C/400°F/gas mark 6.

Prick the potatoes all over with a fork and bake them in the oven until they are soft – about 1 hour.

Cut the kernels off the cobs of corn. Melt half the butter in a small pan, add the kernels and cook gently for 5 minutes. Mix the corn with the fish, chives and seasoning and put to one side.

When the potatoes are cooked, cut them in half lengthways. Scoop out the flesh, leaving a shell, and transfer it to a bowl. Heat the milk in a pan to just below boiling point. Pour the milk on to the potatoes, add the remaining butter and seasoning, and mash.

Place the potato shells on a baking sheet. Divide the corn and fish mixture between the shells. Put 1 tbsp of crème fraîche over each potato and season again.

Pile the mashed potato over each shell. Sprinkle with Cheddar, drizzle with melted butter and bake for 15 minutes, until brown.

pan haggerty

This is my version of a popular favourite. Its strong flavours need a robust meat dish to stand up to it.

serves 2

450g (1lb) medium potatoes, peeled

40ml (1½fl oz) olive oil

25g (1oz) butter

1 red onion, thinly sliced

2 cloves of garlic, crushed

125g (4½oz) Red Leicester cheese, grated

3 tbsp chopped chives

salt and black pepper

Thinly slice the potatoes on a mandolin. Heat the oil and butter in a large frying pan over a medium heat. Remove the pan from the heat and cover the base with a third of the potatoes, followed by a third of the onion slices, a third of the crushed garlic, then a third of the grated cheese, and finally a third of the chives. Season.

Repeat each layer twice. Cover the pan and cook over a gentle heat for about 30 minutes, until everything is soft.

Uncover the pan and brown the pan haggerty under a medium grill until golden brown.

potato gnocchi

Everyone should learn to make gnocchi. It's a messy job, but once you've mastered it you can add all sorts of sauces.

serves 4–6

salt and black pepper

1kg (2lb 4oz) medium waxy potatoes, scrubbed

250–300g (9-10¹/₂oz) plain flour

1 egg

a little nutmeg, grated

40g (1¹/₂oz) butter, plus extra for greasing

Parmesan, grated, to serve

Bring a large pan of salted water to the boil. Add the unpeeled potatoes and boil, lid on, until soft – about 20–25 minutes, depending on the size of the potatoes. Drain in a colander. Peel as soon as possible, while the potatoes are still hot.

Sprinkle about 115g (4oz) of flour over a work surface. Mash the hot, peeled potatoes with a food mill or potato ricer, dropping the potato directly on to the flour. Sprinkle with a further 115g (4oz) flour, reserving the rest for rolling out the gnocchi, and mix lightly into the potatoes.

Break the egg into the mixture, add nutmeg and seasoning to taste, and knead lightly, drawing in more flour as necessary. When the dough is light to the touch and no longer moist or sticky, it is ready to be rolled. Do not overwork it.

Divide the dough into 4 pieces. Flour the surface again, then roll each piece of dough into a sausage about 2cm (³/₄ inches) in diameter, taking care again not to overwork the dough. Cut the rolls into pieces about 2cm (³/₄ inches) long.

Hold a fork in your hand and, one by one, make ridges in each piece of dough with the lines on one side and a hollow on the other side with your thumb.

Bring a large pan of salted water to the boil. When the water is at a fast boil, add about half the gnocchi. When they rise to the surface, after about 3–4 minutes, they are done. Lift out with a draining spoon and transfer to a gratin dish.

Repeat with the remaining gnocchi. When all are cooked, toss the gnocchi with butter and sprinkle with grated Parmesan.

baked beef with a potato crust

This is a really satisfying dish. The marinating and slow cooking of the beef gives the whole dish a really rich flavour.

serves 4

300ml (10fl oz) sherry

3 juniper berries, crushed

1 strip of orange zest

salt and black pepper

700g (1lb 9oz) stewing or braising beef, cut into 2.5cm (1 inch) cubes

3 tbsp vegetable oil

2 onions, quartered

2 carrots, cut into large chunks

1 clove of garlic, crushed

225g (8oz) chestnut mushrooms, wiped and cut into bite-sized pieces

150ml (5fl oz) beef stock

2 tbsp cornflour

for the potato crust

1kg (2lb 4oz) potatoes, peeled and grated

4 tbsp olive oil

4 tbsp creamed horseradish

80g (2³/₄oz) Cheddar, grated

Mix together the sherry, juniper berries and orange zest in a large bowl, then season with pepper. Add the beef and mix well to cover the meat. Cover and leave in the fridge overnight to marinate.

Preheat the oven to 170°C/325°F/gas mark 3. Drain the beef, reserving the marinade and discarding the berries and zest.

Heat the vegetable oil in large ovenproof casserole dish. Add the beef in small batches and fry for a couple of minutes to brown all over. Return all the beef to the casserole dish and add the onions, carrots and garlic. Sweat, lid on, over a medium heat for 5 minutes. Stir in the mushrooms, reserved marinade and the stock.

Mix the cornflour with 3 tbsp of water and stir it into the beef. Season, cover and cook in the oven for 1¹/₂ hours.

Just before the beef is cooked, prepare the potato crust. Bring a pan of salted water to the boil. Drop in the grated potatoes and, as soon as the water comes to the boil again, drain the potatoes in a colander. Squeeze out the excess water and transfer the potatoes to a bowl. Stir in the olive oil, horseradish, Cheddar and salt and pepper to taste.

Remove the beef from the oven and sprinkle over the potato mixture evenly. Increase the temperature to 200°C/400°F/gas mark 6. Bake with the lid off for 30 minutes, then brown under a hot grill for a further 6 minutes.

chips and curry sauce

My good mate Zed reliably informs me that this is the best hangover cure she knows. She should know, she suffers more hangovers that your average army regiment. I just think her curry sauce is the best chip dip I know.

serves 4

50g (1³/₄oz) butter

1 small onion, finely chopped

1 dessert apple, peeled, cored and finely chopped

2 tbsp medium curry powder

3 tbsp plain flour

600ml (1 pint) good bouillon stock such as Marigold

1 tsp curry paste

1 tbsp mango chutney

1 tbsp brown sugar

juice of ¹/₂ lemon

salt

35g (1¹/₄oz) sultanas

Melt the butter in a pan over a medium heat. Add the onion and apple and cook gently for 5 minutes.

Stir in the curry powder and flour. Gradually add the stock and bring to the boil.

Add the remaining ingredients, reduce the heat and simmer, lid on, for 25 minutes.

Meanwhile, cook the chips following the recipe on page 227.

salsify

When you first glance at salsify you could be forgiven for thinking that it's a stick. But don't judge a book by its cover; just under the skin of that dirty stick lies unique-flavoured flesh. I usually see salsify about 30cm (12 inches) long, but I have seen it as long as 75cm (30 inches). It needs a lot of washing, scrubbing and peeling, but it's worth it. Salsify is nearly always sold with a lot of earth attached, which is a good thing. All that earth protects the flesh inside, and more vegetables should be sold this way. The earth has to come off and the skin has to be peeled lightly – and I mean lightly.

The tender flesh, once exposed, discolours alarmingly quickly. The peeled salsify must be kept in acidulated water (water with lemon juice or vinegar added).

For years, salsify has been referred to as the 'oyster vegetable' because of its grey-white colour. I can't imagine it was named 'oyster' because of its flavour – I've heard chefs say that it tastes slightly of oysters, but not to me, it doesn't. I would describe the taste as creamy yet earthy, with an almost nutty aftertaste, and quite unique. It's good to serve these less used vegetables; guests always think you're terribly clever, when in truth such veg are often no harder to prepare and cook than any other. Apparently, botanically speaking, salsify is a member of the daisy family, which makes it a relative of lettuce. What is it with botanists?!

A few extravagant souls don't allow the roots to form on salsify, instead harvesting it as young shoots. I've never been given a salsify shoot so I can't comment, but allegedly it is a great delicacy. I've heard it whispered that the flower buds are delicious, too.

a few facts about salsify

It is very difficult to find the origins of salsify. Botanists think it must have been native to the Mediterranean area. We have evidence of the first cultivation in Italy from the early 16th century, and in England in the late 17th century. It was probably eaten in the classical world, but the earliest surviving mention is from the marvellously named Albertus Magnus in the 13th century. The other point worth noting is that, even though it was grown in England in the 17th century, salsify was almost exclusively grown for its purple flowers. There are no recipes for it until the 18th century.

buying salsify

Press the earth-covered salsify between your fingers; it should be very firm.

storing salsify

Salsify can be kept out of the fridge for up to 10 days. Once peeled, it will be fine in acidulated water for up to 2 days.

| jan | feb | mar | apr | may | jun | jul | aug | sep | oct | nov | dec |

boiling salsify and serving with cream or butter

Top and tail the roots. Using a brush, scrub the salsify under a cold tap, then scrape or carefully peel away the skin, putting the salsify in a bowl of acidulated water as you go. Cut them into thumb-size rounds. Bring a large pan of salted water to the boil. Add the roots and simmer, lid off, for 15–20 minutes, until soft. Add butter or single cream to taste when serving.

Try with: delicate fish.

steaming salsify

Do as above up to and including bringing a large pan of water to the boil. Put the salsify in a sieve and place the colander above the boiling water – it must not touch the water. Put a lid on top. Cook for about 20–30 minutes, until soft. Add butter when serving.

Try with: roast duck.

salsify gratin

As you'll notice in this book, gratin is a real favourite of mine. This one has good, strong autumnal flavours.

serves 4

1 tbsp butter, for greasing

450g (1lb) salsify, scrubbed

juice of ½ lemon

salt and black pepper

450g (1lb) spinach or curly kale, washed and chopped

150ml (5fl oz) chicken stock

300ml (10fl oz) single cream

Preheat the oven to 170°C/325°F/gas mark 3. Grease the inside of a gratin dish with the butter.

Peel the salsify, cut it into 5cm (2 inch) lengths and drop the pieces into water acidulated with lemon juice as you go. Drain when you are ready to use it.

Bring a pan of salted water to the boil. Drop in the drained salsify and cook for about 10 minutes, until just tender. Drain again.

Meanwhile, put the greens in a large pan with just the water left clinging to them after washing, and cook for about 3 minutes, until wilted.

Put the stock, cream and seasoning in a small pan and heat gently until it is near simmering point, stirring.

Arrange the greens and salsify in the greased gratin dish. Pour over the cream mixture and bake for 45 minutes to 1 hour, until brown and bubbling.

samphire

Samphire is juicy, pleasantly salty and has a very nice crunch. It requires very little cooking and is perfect with a piece of fish balanced on top, which is perhaps why so many fishmongers sell it. This wild plant is found in salty marshes near the coast (it is denser near to estuaries), and yet it is sometimes mistakenly sold as seaweed. It is available from mid-spring throughout the summer. I know of no samphire farms in Britain, but there must be some in North Africa because a huge amount finds its way over here from Egypt.

boiling samphire

Wash the samphire under cold water. Bring a pan of unsalted water to the boil. Drop in the samphire and boil, lid off, for about 2 minutes. Drain well, then reheat in a pan to which you have added a knob of butter.

Try with: grilled or poached haddock.

samphire and salmon with a crème fraîche sauce

It's a toss-up as to whether the samphire or the salmon steals the show with this dish. Veg lovers like me would suggest that the salmon is just giving a bit of colour and a different texture to a plate of samphire.

serves 4

500g (1lb 2oz) samphire
100g (3¹/₂oz) butter
2 tbsp olive oil
4 x 150g (5¹/₂oz) salmon fillets, skinned
a little plain flour, seasoned
black pepper
8 tbsp crème fraîche
2 tbsp chopped chives

Remove any woody roots from the samphire and wash it well. Bring a pan of unsalted water to the boil, add the samphire and boil, lid off, for 2 minutes. Drain in a sieve, pushing the veg against the sides with a wooden spoon.

Melt half the butter with the oil in a frying pan over a medium heat. Coat the salmon lightly with the seasoned flour, then pat it to remove any excess flour. When the butter and oil mixture is hot, drop in the fish and fry until it has coloured four-fifths from the top. Now turn the fish over and cook completely.

Meanwhile, melt the remaining butter in a clean pan. Add the samphire and plenty of pepper and warm it over a gentle heat.

Warm the crème fraîche in a fourth pan and add 1 tbsp chives.

To serve, place a quarter of the samphire on each plate. Put a salmon fillet on top and spoon some crème fraîche sauce over the fish. Serve scattered with extra chopped chives.

jan   feb   mar   apr   may   jun   jul   aug   sep   oct   nov   dec

spinach

What I love about spinach is that it's so easy to eat.
It hardly needs chewing at times. I also love that
slight iron taste you get with leafy green veg that lets
you know every mouthful is doing you good. It just
feels right. It's strong but not bitter. I'm fond of
Indian restaurants (I believe the local Indian has
a place in our hearts, very much like the local pub),
and sag aloo (spinach with potatoes) is one of my
favourite side dishes. Spinach is also incredibly easy
to cook: just grab a handful of it, stick it in a pan
and in seconds the leaves and stems are releasing
their own perfectly seasoned cooking liquid.

The only problem, of course, is that because spinach has such a high water content and so little weight, it reduces a lot. There are varieties of spinach that have more robust and rubbery leaves, rather like a soft Savoy cabbage, which don't reduce as much as some thinner varieties. But you don't have to use these if you don't want to – just make sure you buy enough. In fairness to spinach, it is far richer in protein than any other leafy vegetable.

baby spinach

Pousse (baby spinach) is harvested young and immature. It is used mainly as a salad leaf, and I think it is perfect for the job – it is inexpensive, and it can make up the bulk of your salad. Use it as a base and scatter more expensive leaves on top of it. Pousse will only stand very little cooking and is virtually always served cold; if you are going to cook it, do it very quickly; just introduce it to the heat. So, pousse meets pan, pan meets pousse, and that's about it.

a few facts about spinach

Spinach originated in the heart of the Persian Empire, and was introduced to Europe in the 11th century via the Arab invasions of southern Spain. The 12th-century Arab writer Ibn al-Awam gave it the title 'prince of vegetables'. The name 'spinach' is certainly Persian in origin (the Persian name being '*aspanākh*'). The vegetable travelled eastwards from Persia with far more success than it did westwards.

Spinach took a long time to become established as a food type in Britain. It was seen very much as a novelty item, enjoying a reputation as an exotic and fashionable food along with sugar (a hugely expensive rarity in the 17th century). It was originally used in Britain primarily for medicinal purposes.

buying spinach

Look out for big leaves. This has nothing to do with flavour or freshness; it's just about the prepping time if you plan to remove the stalks (although I like the stalks as long as they're not too big). I'm never a fan of veg sold in sealed plastic bags; if you can buy the leaves loose in a box, stick your hand in and have a bit of a rummage. If they are big, thick and very fresh, they will squeak slightly as you move them around.

jan	feb	mar	apr	may	jun	jul	aug	sep	oct	nov	dec

Look out for any wetness around the edge of the leaf, as this is a sure sign that the veg is dying.

storing spinach
Store in a fridge for a maximum of 2 days.

steaming spinach
Wash the spinach very well and, if it is large leaved, pull off the stalks. Place the leaves in a large pot. Cook the spinach over a gentle heat, turning the leaves all the time until they have wilted – this should take no more than 2–3 minutes. Do not use any additional water, just what the leaves have been washed in. Once the spinach has wilted, cook for a further minute. Drain if necessary. Season. If you prefer, stir in a large lump of butter when cooked.
Try with: liver.

cooking spinach in cream
Prepare the spinach as for steaming. When it is cooked, drain well, squeezing the leaves against the sides of a colander using a wooden spoon. Chop up the spinach finely and return it to a frying pan with a knob of butter and some double cream or crème fraîche to taste and heat through.
Try with: fish.

spinach and Roquefort tart

Is this ever a winner? It is easy, light and rich (unlike me). Go on, make this, I beg you. Everyone always seems terribly impressed by tarts. In fact, I make two at a time – I always demolish one before it's cooled.

serves 4

500g (1lb 2oz) ready-rolled puff pastry

25g (1oz) butter

1 red onion, finely sliced

125g (4½oz) spinach, leaf only

150g (5½oz) Roquefort cheese

100g (3½oz) mascarpone cheese

4 eggs

black pepper

Push the pastry evenly into a tart dish, lining the base and walls, then trim. Prick the base. Refrigerate for at least 2 hours.

Preheat the oven to 180°C/350°F/gas mark 4.

Melt the butter in a pan over a low heat and add the onion. Cook slowly, lid on, for 10 minutes.

Add the spinach and cook, stirring regularly. After 2 minutes it should be wilted. Remove from the heat and allow to cool.

Mix the Roquefort and mascarpone together in a bowl. Add the eggs and pepper and whisk well. Add this to the cooled spinach.

Pour the mixture into the tart and bake for 45 minutes.

spinach turnovers

Spinach, anchovy, pine nuts and raisins make a great combination, and these pies are both tasty and satisfying.

makes 20

1 tbsp olive oil, plus extra for greasing

25g (1oz) raisins

450g (1lb) spinach, washed and chopped

6 anchovy fillets, chopped

2 cloves of garlic, finely chopped

salt and black pepper

1 tbsp chopped basil

25g (1oz) pine nuts, chopped

350g (12oz) puff pastry

1 egg, beaten

Preheat the oven to 180°C/350°F/gas mark 4. Grease 2 baking sheets with olive oil. Soak the raisins in warm water for 15 minutes. Drain and chop.

Heat the olive oil in a wok over a low heat. Add the spinach and cook for 2 minutes. Turn up the heat and evaporate any liquid. Stir in the anchovies, garlic, seasoning and basil and cook for 1 minute. Add the chopped raisins and pine nuts, stir, then set aside to cool.

Roll out the pastry to 3mm (⅛ inch) thick. Using a 7.5cm (3 inch) round cutter, cut out 20 rounds of pastry, re-rolling as necessary.

Place about 2 tsp of the filling in the middle of each pastry round. Brush the edges of the pastry with water. Fold over the sides of pastry and seal well. Brush each pie with beaten egg and bake on the baking sheets for about 20–25 minutes.

eggs florentine

This is a breakfast dish, or a brunch if you're too lazy to get up from the night before. Soft poached egg oozing on to spinach is a vision worthy of oil and canvas.

serves 4

50g (1³/₄oz) butter

750g (1lb 10oz) spinach, washed and drained

75ml (2¹/₂fl oz) double cream

a few gratings of nutmeg

salt and black pepper

4 eggs

1 tbsp freshly grated Parmesan

2 pinches of cayenne

for the cheese sauce

25g (1oz) butter

300ml (10fl oz) full-fat milk

25g (1oz) plain flour

115g (4oz) Gruyère, grated

a few gratings of nutmeg

Preheat the oven to 200°C/400°F/gas mark 6. Butter a large gratin dish or 4 small ones with 1 tbsp of butter.

Place the spinach in a large pan with just the water it was washed in, and cook over a medium heat for 2–3 minutes, until wilted. Drain well, squeezing to remove the excess liquid. Chop it finely.

Return the chopped spinach to the pan, add the remaining butter, cream, nutmeg and seasoning and mix well. Place in the gratin dish or dishes. Make hollows for the eggs in the spinach.

For the cheese sauce, heat the butter in 1 small pan and the milk in another. Add the flour to the butter and cook for 1 minute. Gradually pour in the warm milk, whisking all the time. Cook for 3 minutes, stirring or whisking constantly. Remove from the heat and add three quarters of the Gruyère as well as the nutmeg. Stir.

Bring a large pan of salted water to the boil. Carefully crack in each egg and poach in boiling water for 4 minutes. Drain well.

Place an egg in each hollow of spinach. Cover with cheese sauce and sprinkle with the remaining Gruyère, the Parmesan and the cayenne. Bake for 10 minutes, until golden.

spinach and mushroom pancakes

Spinach and mushrooms are a classic and irresistible combination. These pancakes are a great way of getting the kids to eat spinach!

serves 4

100g (3½oz) spinach, washed and stalks removed

100g (3½oz) plain flour

salt and black pepper

1 egg

300ml (10fl oz) milk

25g (1oz) butter

1 shallot, finely chopped

350g (12oz) flat mushrooms, sliced

1 tsp chopped tarragon

2 tbsp crème fraîche

50g (1¾oz) Cheddar, grated

Put the spinach in a pan with the water still clinging to it from washing. Cook over a medium heat for 2–3 minutes, until wilted. Drain well. Chop half the cooked spinach and put the other half to one side.

Put the flour in a large bowl and add a pinch of salt. Break in the egg. Gradually pour in the milk, whisking all the time until you have a smooth batter. Add the chopped spinach. Pour into a jug. Refrigerate for half an hour or so.

Melt a little of the butter in a frying pan over a medium heat. When the butter is hot, pour in just enough batter to coat the pan, tilting the pan to and fro. Cook the pancake until it moves freely, then turn it over and cook until both sides are golden. Keep to one side, covered, while you make the rest of the pancakes.

Melt the rest of the butter in a large frying pan over a medium heat. When the butter is hot, add the shallot and fry gently for 5 minutes. Turn the heat right up and add the mushrooms and tarragon – you want the heat to be high enough to evaporate the liquid from the mushrooms. After 5 minutes, add the crème fraîche and the remaining spinach. Stir and instantly remove from the heat.

Put a pancake on a flat surface. Add some filling to one-quarter of the pancake. Fold the pancake in half from left to right, then fold it in half from top to bottom.

Put the filled pancakes in an ovenproof dish. Sprinkle over the cheese and place them under a medium grill until the cheese has completely melted.

baby spinach and chicken liver salad

I have always enjoyed chicken livers. Baby spinach is perfect with them, as it doesn't compete for strength of flavour, makes the whole dish refreshing and adds colour to the plate. This dressing uses strong spices but in relatively small amounts.

serves 4

500g (1lb 2oz) chicken livers

2 tbsp olive oil

25g (1oz) butter

6 rashers of streaky bacon, cubed

2 cloves of garlic, finely sliced

¹/₄ tsp ground cumin

¹/₄ tsp ground coriander

¹/₄ tsp powdered cinnamon

salt and black pepper

6 tbsp sherry vinegar

knob of fresh ginger, grated

200g (7oz) baby spinach, washed and dried

Trim the chicken livers and slice to bite size. Heat the oil and butter in a frying pan over a high heat. Add the bacon. Sizzle for 2 minutes, then add the garlic. Cook for a further couple of minutes, until just coloured, stirring all the time. Add the spices, whilst stirring, and fry for another minute.

Reduce the heat a little, add the chicken livers, season, and cook for about 3–4 minutes, tossing the pan frequently – you want the livers to be crusty outside, but still pink on the inside. Using a slotted spoon, take the livers out of the pan and set aside. Add the vinegar and ginger to the pan and bring to the boil. Return the livers to the pan and cook, stirring, until hot.

Divide the spinach between the plates and serve the liver mixture on top, not forgetting the hot dressing.

baby spinach, watercress and orange salad

You can make this any time of the year. It has sharpness and sweetness in equal measure and is so easy to make it hurts. The hardest thing is preparing the orange segments.

serves 4

100g (3½oz) baby spinach, washed and dried

100g (3½oz) watercress, washed and dried

3 oranges

for the dressing

1 tbsp Dijon mustard

1 tbsp runny honey

4 tbsp olive oil

4 tbsp red wine vinegar

2 tbsp chopped chives

salt and black pepper

Mix the spinach and watercress in a big bowl.

Make the dressing by mixing the mustard, honey, olive oil, vinegar and chives. Season.

Slice the top and bottom from each orange so that it sits flat on the chopping board. With a sharp, small knife, cut away the skin and pith from top to bottom in slices, curving with the orange.

Holding the skinned orange in one hand, carefully cut out each segment by slicing down inside the line of the white pith – do this over a bowl to save juice.

Combine the orange segments and juice with the dressing and pour this over the leaves.

squash and pumpkin

Squashes have been with us for a long time and I don't quite understand why they're not more popular. Perhaps we only associate them with carving. Or maybe people are scared of their size. There are many small varieties to practise cooking with; I would suggest an onion or acorn variety. Perhaps, with so many varieties, people are unsure as to the right type for them. I will go into varieties and the difference in the flesh later, although the difference is subtle. All winter squashes will cook in the same way; they will bake, roast or mash. They make superb soups. So stop worrying, go on, enjoy.

Sometimes the reasons why you like a meal aren't all about the food – a lot depends on how hungry or relaxed you are. My favourite pumpkin meal was cooked by my mate from Radio 4's *Veg Talk*, Charlie Hicks. We were filming on a cold allotment in Liverpool. Charlie hollowed out a pumpkin and cooked a spicy chicken stew in it. I love that man. Versatile thing, the squash.

Pumpkins and squashes are from the cucurbit family, which also includes the cucumber. When you think about the skins and types of flesh, the family connection doesn't seem far-fetched. For cooks, not horticulturalists, squashes fall into 2 categories: winter and summer. The main difference between the 2 is the thickness of the skin. A summer squash only requires a thin skin to protect it from the elements; a winter squash needs a thicker skin. So sometimes, especially when roasting, a summer squash can be cooked and eaten in slices with the skin still on. Not so with winter; this needs its skin cut off before cooking. Big biceps at the ready.

Loads of people grow squashes in their allotments. I once filmed with a champion pumpkin grower (oh, the exciting life I lead). This guy was a plumber by trade. He had rigged up under-soil heating on his allotment and had monsters trailing out of his greenhouse. He still has a long way to go, the record books have a 450kg (992lb) specimen. That is nearly a pallet of spuds!

types of squash

There are literally scores of different squashes. They come in myriad shapes, sizes and colours. This makes referencing them very difficult, especially when the same squash not only has a different name country by country, but sometimes town by town as well.

Every year I have a hell of a job explaining to chefs over the phone the difference in variety. The confusion multiplies when a head chef decides to give one of them a new name and all his staff copy his example.

winter squash

jan	feb	mar	apr	may	jun	jul	aug	sep	oct	nov	dec

summer squash

jan	feb	mar	apr	may	jun	jul	aug	sep	oct	nov	dec

Winter squashes are squashes that are allowed to mature on the vine and that are then stored for use in the winter. The skin is hard and not to be eaten, but the flesh can taste fantastic – I think much better than most varieties of summer squashes. Some good regular winter varieties are **Delicata**, **Hubbard**, **Kabocha** and **onion**.

The **pumpkin** is the most celebrated of the winter squashes. Most of the pumpkins I see on sale at Hallowe'en are awful; they seem mostly to be **étample** or **jackpot** varieties. These may carve beautifully, but are nowhere near the best eaters. Straight after Hallowe'en is the best time to buy pumpkins and squashes; greengrocers have stands full of them and are desperate to find them a home.

It saddens me to say this, but probably the most common squash at our table is the **butternut**. Of all the squashes available to us all year, we pick on the one that is the most difficult to grow in northern Europe, and so is very often imported.

Summer squashes are eaten fresh, in the summer season, when they are immature on the vine and the skin is still soft. Good summer varieties include **scallop** and **crookneck**. **Acorn** is a good summer variety, although it is often stored and used as a winter squash. Marrows and courgettes are officially varieties of summer squash, but they are used in such different ways to most of the squashes we eat that I have given them their own chapter in this book.

a few facts about pumpkins and squash

The name pumpkin comes from the French '*pompon*', taken from the classical Greek '*pepon*', meaning melon. Squashes originated in America and are, in fact, some of the earliest known crops to be harvested by original Americans, north and south (squash seeds have been found in Mexican burial graves dating back to 8,000BC). By the time Columbus brought squashes over to Europe, Indians were successfully growing them all along the east coast of America, right the way up to Canada. Many New World foods took some time to enter the Old World, but not squashes; they were being grown in Europe just 50 years after Columbus' arrival.

buying pumpkins and squashes

Choose veg with firm, dry skin – absolutely no wet bits. Different colours are fine but damp patches are out. Summer squashes are in season August to mid September, but can last right up to December if stored well; winter squashes are in season September to February, but again can last up to April if well stored. Anything you buy outside of these months will almost certainly have been imported.

storing winter squashes

If whole, pumpkins and squashes keep well in a cool dark place. The flesh will successfully freeze after cooking in a pan with a little water.

boiling winter squashes

Halve the squash and scoop out the seeds using a metal spoon. Cut the base off the halves, then cut the halves into manageable shapes. Slice off the skin. Cut the flesh into chunks the size of Lego bricks. Bring a pan of salted water to the boil. Add the squash and boil, lid off, until soft (5–10 minutes depending on size). Drain.
Try with: meat pies.

braising winter squashes

Halve the squash and scoop out the seeds using a metal spoon. Cut the base off the halves, then cut the halves into manageable shapes. Slice off the skin. Put the pieces in a pie dish. Cover with chicken stock, add a knob of butter, a squeeze of lemon and a sliced clove of garlic. Cook in an oven preheated to 180°C/350°F/gas mark 4 for 1 hour.
Try with: pork chops.

griddling winter squashes

Halve the squash and scoop out the seeds using a spoon. Cut the base off the halves, then cut the halves into manageable shapes. Slice off the skin. Cut the flesh into 5mm (1/4 inch) slices and cook in a pan of boiling salted water for 6 minutes. When soft, drain. Return to the pan and heat for 1 minute to remove the excess liquid. Heat a griddle pan, drizzle olive oil into the pan and griddle the squash for 2 minutes on each side.
Try this: drunk in the garden.

puréeing winter squashes

Halve the squash and scoop out the seeds using a spoon. Cut the base off the halves, then cut the halves into manageable shapes. Slice off the skin. Cut the flesh into 5mm (1/4 inch) slices and cook in a pan of boiling salted water for 6 minutes. Drain. Return to the pan and heat for 1 minute to remove the excess liquid. Add some black pepper to the pan with 50g (1¾oz) of butter to every 500g (1lb 2oz) of flesh. Roughly blitz with a hand-held blender – it should not be too smooth. Gently reheat for 1 minute.
Try with: cold meats.

pan-finishing winter squashes

Halve the squash and scoop out the seeds using a metal spoon. Cut the base off the halves, then cut the halves into manageable shapes. Slice off the skin. Cut the flesh into chunks the size of Lego bricks. Bring a pan of salted water to the boil. Add the squash and boil, lid off, until soft (5–10 minutes depending on size). Drain. Return to the pan and heat for 1 minute to remove the excess liquid. Melt some butter in the pan with the squash and toss together for 1 minute.

Try with: sausages.

roasting winter squashes

Halve the squash and scoop out the seeds using a metal spoon. Cut the base off the halves, then cut the halves into manageable shapes. Slice off the skin. Cut flesh into 5mm (¼ inch) slices and put them in a roasting tin. Drizzle with olive oil and sprinkle with salt and pepper. Cook in an oven preheated to 180°C/350°F/gas mark 4 until soft (10–20 minutes).

Try with: roast meats.

seeds

Keep the seeds when you scoop out your squash or pumpkin; they make a more than decent nibble. You have to wash the pith away from them first, then stick them on a baking tray in an oven preheated to 150°C/300°F/gas mark 2 for 15 minutes. Put them in a bowl and add some salt.

Try with: beer.

squash fondue

This is perfect for a party. You can adapt the recipe using cheeses that you love. Also, you can use a big pumpkin for group fondues, or a little one to serve 2.

serves 2

1 squash, approx. 1kg (2lb 4oz)

140g (5oz) Emmental cheese, grated

140g (5oz) Gruyère cheese, grated

1 clove of garlic, crushed

1 tbsp plain flour

175ml (6fl oz) white wine

1 tsp lemon juice

1 tbsp Kirsch

6 grates of nutmeg

salt and black pepper

Preheat the oven to 170°C/325°F/gas mark 3.

Cut a lid from the squash, with the knife pointing towards the stalk. You need to cut the lid in such a way that it will not fall inside when cooking. Remove the seeds with a spoon and discard.

Combine the grated cheeses and crushed garlic with the flour and put it into a heavy pot with the wine, lemon juice, Kirsch, nutmeg and seasoning.

Melt over a very low heat, stirring occasionally. Once it has melted and is creamy, pour it into the squash. Replace the lid.

Place on a baking tray and bake for 1½ hrs. Serve with a dark loaf such as rye bread.

pumpkin soup

Soups are winter food, and pumpkin makes a pleasingly sweet soup. You've got to have that drizzle of truffle oil with this – a drizzle, that's all. Don't be greedy, you can have too much of a good thing. At the end of the day, you do want to taste the pumpkin flesh.

serves 2

2 tbsp sunflower oil

25g (1oz) butter

1 onion, finely sliced

1 potato, sliced

500g (1lb 2oz) chopped pumpkin flesh, no skin no seed

1.2 litres (2 pints) chicken stock

1 clove of garlic, crushed

4 tsp truffle oil

Heat the oil and butter in a pan over a low heat. Add the onion, potato and pumpkin, and sweat, lid on, for about 15 minutes, until the vegetables are soft. Stir regularly; do not allow them to brown.

Add the chicken stock and garlic. Simmer, with no lid, for about 20 minutes, until the veg can be easily pierced with a fork.

Blitz the soup and push it through a sieve. Serve in bowls with a swirl of truffle oil on top.

swede

Swede is a supreme winter vegetable. Pound for pound, it is serious value for money and it will store uncut for months. Roast swede is a fine thing, but I like this veg best boiled and mashed with lots of butter and the smallest amount of nutmeg. Swede means winter. Steaming hot and buttery, it is exactly what you need after a long walk on a cold winter's day. Known as a root vegetable, the swede is not actually a root, but the swollen base of a stem. It is closely related to the turnip, which probably explains why the Scots call both swedes and turnips 'neeps'.

I see the swede as a mini kitchen workout. Cutting through one of those tough blighters is seriously hard work. Forget 20 minutes on the treadmill; just slice up 5kg (11lb) of swede.

types of swede

Most swedes have an orange-yellow flesh and yellow skin, while some have a white skin with splashes of purple. They are all very fibrous and need a lot of cooking. Although related to the turnip, they are much milder in taste, and small, young ones are usually much milder than bigger ones.

a few facts about swede

In *The Oxford Companion to Food*, Alan Davidson says swede probably originated in central Europe, while Larousse claims it originated in Scandinavia. Well, in the great scheme of things, looking down at a map of the world, it's not that far away, is it? For such a good, hardy winter crop, the swede has amazingly not been around for very long; it didn't reach England until the 17th century, and it didn't become a mainstream veg here until the 18th century. It finally got to America in the 19th century. The American name for the swede is 'rutabaga', which is a corruption of the Swedish term '*rota bagge*', meaning 'red bags', referring of course to its bulbous shape.

buying swede

Avoid any swede with cracks or broken bits and look out for little holes, as this indicates worm damage.

storing swede

Swedes store fantastically. Kept in the cool, or even in the fridge, they will be more than happy for up to 2 months.

mashing swede

Peel the swede, then chop it into 2cm (¾ inch) cubes. Bring a pan of salted water to the boil. Add the swede and boil, lid on, for about 20 minutes, until soft. Do not boil too hard as root veg will break up with rough handling. Drain well, return to the pan

| jan | feb | mar | apr | may | jun | jul | aug | sep | oct | nov | dec |

and mash it up, keeping it as rough as you can handle. Add butter and salt, to taste, and lots of pepper, then stir – the amount of butter you use depends on what texture you are searching for.

Try with: haggis – this makes a perfect combination.

roasting swede

Preheat the oven to 190°C/375°F/gas mark 5. Peel the swede, then chop it into roast-potato-size chunks. Bring a pan of salted water to the boil. Add the swede and boil, lid on, for about 5 minutes. Drain. Preheat 1cm (½ inch) of vegetable oil in a roasting tin. Carefully add the swede chunks to the hot oil. Roast for 40–50 minutes, turning occasionally.

Try with: your Sunday joint.

vegetable and lentil casserole

You know, I'm a big carnivore. That said, I demolished a big bowl of this casserole one hungry night and didn't even notice there was no meat in it. This is a hearty dish.

serves 6

1 tbsp vegetable oil

25g (1oz) butter

2 leeks, sliced

2 cloves of garlic, crushed

4 stalks celery, sliced

2 carrots, diced

2 parsnips, diced

1 sweet potato, diced

225g (8oz) swede, diced

175g (6oz) lentils

1 x 400g tin tomatoes

1 tbsp each of thyme and oregano

2 bay leaves

850ml (1¹/₂ pints) vegetable stock

salt and black pepper

1 tbsp cornflour

Preheat the oven to 180°C/350°F/gas mark 4.

Heat the oil and butter in an ovenproof casserole dish over a low to medium heat. When it is hot, add the leeks, garlic and celery and fry gently for 3 minutes.

Add the carrots, parsnips, sweet potato, swede, lentils, tomatoes, herbs, stock and seasoning, then stir well and bring to the boil.

Cover and bake in the oven for 50 minutes, until the vegetables are soft. Stir the casserole a couple of times during cooking.

Remove from the oven. Blend the cornflour with 2 tbsp of water to make a paste. Stir this into the casserole. Simmer for 5 minutes and serve.

root vegetable gratin

A bit of work goes into making this, but the resulting array of flavour is worth the effort.

serves 4

2 large potatoes

1 large parsnip

150g (5¹/₂oz) swede

25g (1oz) butter

1 tbsp vegetable oil

2 cloves of garlic, crushed

2 tbsp Dijon mustard

1 tbsp lemon juice

1 tbsp thyme leaves

125ml (4fl oz) vegetable stock

salt and black pepper

Preheat the oven to 200°C/400°F/gas mark 6. After peeling, slice the potatoes, parsnip and swede thinly using a mandolin.

Heat the butter and oil in a frying pan over a medium heat. Add the garlic and fry for 3 minutes. Stir in the mustard, lemon juice and thyme. Add the stock and mix well. Bring to the boil, then remove from the heat and pour the liquid into a heatproof jug.

Place a layer of the veg over the base of an ovenproof pot. Season and pour over some of the liquid. Keep doing this until all the veg and liquid is used up. Season the top layer. Cover with baking parchment and bake for 1 hour. Remove the paper and return to the oven for 15 minutes, until golden.

lamb pasties

Everyone should know how to make a pasty. They can look very pretty, but if, like me, you don't want to spend time crimping the edges then that's fine, too.

serves 4

1 tbsp vegetable oil

225g (8oz) minced lamb

1 clove of garlic, crushed

1 small onion, finely chopped

60g (2¹/₄oz) carrots, diced

50g (1³/₄oz) celery, diced

60g (2¹/₄oz) swede, diced

60g (2¹/₄oz) parsnips, diced

¹/₂ tsp rosemary leaves

¹/₂ tsp chopped sage

salt and black pepper

1 tbsp plain flour

225ml (8fl oz) strong lamb stock

1 medium potato, boiled in its skin and diced

1 tbsp soy sauce

500g (1lb 2oz) shortcrust pastry

1 egg, beaten

Heat the oil in a large frying pan over a high heat. When the oil is hot, add the lamb and cook until it has some colour. Add the garlic, onion, carrots, celery, swede, parsnips and herbs. Cover and sweat for 10 minutes.

Season well, stir in the flour and cook, stirring occasionally, for 3 minutes. Stir in the stock and cook, lid on, for a further 10 minutes. Add the potato and cook, lid on, for another 5 minutes. Add the soy sauce and check the seasoning. Leave to cool completely.

Preheat the oven to 200°C/400°F/gas mark 6.

Roll out the pastry and cut it into 4 x 15cm (6 inch) rounds using a side plate. Spoon a quarter of the filling on to each pastry round and brush the edges with beaten egg. Fold the pastry over the filling to make triangles. Pinch the edges all around to seal in the filling and crimp them with your thumbs, if you wish. Place on a baking sheet, brush with beaten egg and bake for 30 minutes.

sweetcorn

I have loved corn on the cob for as long as I can remember. My mum (although loving, warm and very funny) wasn't a great cook. A lot of children are suspicious of vegetables, but if they'd had my culinary upbringing, they'd be even more nervous! I can clearly remember my first ever cob. Its bright, glistening yellow kernels looked wonderful, but I was dubious. As soon as I nibbled off that first kernel I was hooked – never before had a vegetable released such sweet juice, and it was all coated in salty butter. It's still a flavour I never tire of.

Charles Secrett, the man who owns the farm where I work, shares my love of corn. The flavour of a vegetable deteriorates as soon as you pick it (it's dying as soon as it's picked), so Charles swears the best thing to do is boil a pot of water next to a field of corn, rip off a big ear, and sprint over to the pot as fast as you can.

The sweetcorn we know is a variety of maize, one of the most important crops in the world, and maize is a type of grass. As far as I know, only the Brits and Americans eat corn on the cob. In France they use it as food for chickens. Lucky old chickens!

Of course, sweetcorn is a New World crop that loves hot weather, so it thrives in Spain, southern France, Italy and Portugal. It is popular in North and Latin America, and there are many alternative shapes and colours; I've even seen a purple corn.

We learned the joy of cob-eating from our North American cousins. Southern Europeans saw it as a new cereal, and in the Veneto they turned it into polenta. Cornmeal, cornflour, polenta, hominy grits and popcorn all come from the same corn or maize plant. Of these, I would only consider eating polenta, cornflour and popcorn. Popcorn is a small variety of corn, and cornflour is the powdered white starch of the corn used as a thickening agent.

baby corn

Baby corn is immature corn, but it has been bred to be harvested when immature. Corn grown for cobs won't give you an edible baby corn. I have no idea who came up with the idea of growing a tiny corn cob – it has to be one of the silliest vegetables known to man. The whole point of the cob is that it's juicy. This little blighter has about as much juice as your average sock and a texture not unlike it. The only use I can think of for it is as an ear-cleaner. I've heard people say they are great in stir-fries, but I can't agree.

a few facts about sweetcorn

Nikolai Vavilov, the great Russian botanist who convinced the Politburo it would be a good idea to fund a worldwide plant-hunting expedition, believed maize originated in the Andes and then spread to Mexico. It is believed maize was grown in Mexico around 7,000BC. Originally a plant with a tiny head, Mayan and Incan farmers developed the big cobs we know now. In 1612 Captain John Smith, leader of the early Virginia colonists, saved the people from starvation by bartering for corn with the native Americans.

jan	feb	mar	apr	may	jun	jul	aug	sep	oct	nov	dec

buying sweetcorn

Avoid peeled cobs in polystyrene and plastic packets; instead buy cobs with the green husk surrounding them. If you can, peel back the husk on at least one of them and ensure the kernels underneath are plump and juicy, with no spots or missing kernels.

storing sweetcorn

With the husk on, the corn will last twice as long as it does unpeeled – anything up to a week (although it's much better eaten straightaway). Keep in a cool, dark place.

preparing raw sweetcorn kernels

Remove the husk from the cob – you must get rid of all the stringy bits. Cut off the point and base. Hold the cob upright and run a sharp knife down the white stem, keeping it as close to the stem as possible so the kernels break off.
Try: in salads.

boiling sweetcorn kernels

Follow the instructions for preparing raw sweetcorn. Bring a large pan of salted water to the boil. Add the sweetcorn and boil, lid off, for about 5 minutes, until soft. Drain well in a colander.
Try with: a mountain of butter.

boiling sweetcorn on the cob

Remove the husk from the cob – you must get rid of all the stringy bits. Cut off the point and base. Bring a large pan of salted water to the boil. Add the sweetcorn and boil, lid off, for about 12 minutes, until soft.
Try with: another mountain of butter.

griddling sweetcorn

Remove the husk from the cob – you must get rid of all the stringy bits. Cut off the point and base. Bring a large pan of salted water to the boil. Add the sweetcorn and boil, lid off, for about 12 minutes. Drain well. Heat a griddle pan over a high heat and brush the sweetcorn with vegetable oil. Add the corn and cook, turning, for 6 minutes. You can also grill or barbecue sweetcorn, but I wouldn't recommend it.
Try with: 2 mountains of butter.

corn and haddock chowder

Not for the faint hearted this one, a chowder is the daddy of soups. I always make loads of this. A big bowl left in my fridge diminishes over a day or two. This is comfort eating. Forget popcorn, this is the perfect accompaniment to a good film.

serves 4

2 sweetcorn cobs

2 potatoes

2 tbsp olive oil

25g (1oz) butter

1 onion, finely chopped

1 stalk celery, finely chopped

300ml (10fl oz) fish stock

100ml (3¹/₂fl oz) white wine

300g (10¹/₂oz) undyed haddock, skinned and cut into 2.5cm (1 inch) chunks

100ml (3¹/₂fl oz) double cream

black pepper

bunch of parsley, chopped

Hold the cobs upright and slice off the yellow kernels.

Quarter the potatoes and slice each quarter into 5. Keep the slices in cold water.

Heat the oil and butter in a large heavy bottomed pan over a low heat. Add the onion and celery and cook, lid on, for 5 minutes.

Add the corn kernels and potatoes and cook, lid on, for 10 minutes, stirring occasionally. Don't break up the potatoes.

Pour in the fish stock and wine, put the lid on, turn up the heat and bring to the boil. Reduce the heat and simmer for 5 minutes.

Add the fish, bring to the boil, then simmer, lid on, for 3 minutes, until the fish is cooked. Remove from the heat.

Stir in the cream and tons of black pepper. Serve in bowls and sprinkle with chopped parsley.

sweetcorn and chicken soup

People often ask me what my favourite restaurant is. If my favourite is the one I dine at the most, then it has to be Ying's Chinese over the road. I am there at least once a week. Ying is a top man, grows veg and is a skilful cook. Here's my attempt at a Chinese classic.

serves 4

100g (3¹/₂oz) chicken breast, skinned and cubed

2 tbsp light soy sauce

1 tbsp medium sherry

1 tsp cornflour

1 tsp sesame oil

2 tbsp vegetable oil

1 tsp grated fresh ginger

1 litre (1³/₄ pints) chicken stock

175g (6oz) sweetcorn kernels

250g (9oz) tinned sweetcorn, blitzed with 1 tbsp of the liquid

2 eggs, beaten

3 spring onions, green parts only, finely chopped, to garnish

Mince the chicken in a food processor; don't overdo it. Place the chicken, soy sauce, sherry, cornflour, 2 tbsp of water and the sesame oil in a bowl and stir. Leave for about 10 minutes.

Heat a wok over a medium to high heat. Add the vegetable oil. When it is hot, add the ginger and fry for 10 seconds. Add the stock, the fresh and blitzed sweetcorn, and heat to just below boiling point.

Measure 6 tbsp of the hot liquid and add it to the chicken mixture, then stir until smooth. Add the chicken mixture to the wok and bring the whole lot to the boil, stirring all the time. Simmer for 5–8 minutes, until the chicken is cooked.

Slowly pour the beaten eggs into the soup whilst stirring. Serve immediately with chopped green spring onions as a garnish.

sweetcorn fritters with *foie gras*

This is the best partner for *foie gras*. The sweetcorn adds a hint of sweetness, but it in no way tries to compete with the liver. The fat from the liver drips into the soft waiting arms of the fritter. I first ate something like this at Kensington Place, where Rowley Leigh calls his fritter a pancake. He's a lot posher than me!

serves 4

2 sweetcorn cobs
125g (4½oz) plain flour
salt
1 egg
25g (1oz) butter, melted
200ml (7fl oz) milk
1 tbsp vegetable oil
enough foie gras for 4 people

Hold the cobs upright and slice off the yellow kernels. Bring a pan of salted water to the boil. Add the kernels and cook for 5 minutes. Drain and set aside.

Mix the flour and 2 pinches of salt in a bowl. Add the egg and melted butter. Whisk in the milk to make a batter and add the corn.

Heat 1 tsp of the oil in a frying pan over a medium heat. Pour enough mixture into the oiled pan to make a fritter the size you want. Cook until it has browned on one side, then turn and brown on the other side. Use the remaining oil to cook the rest of the fritters. You need 4.

Meanwhile, heat a dry frying pan for the *foie gras*. Slice off as much as your heart can cope with. As soon as you turn the fritter, put the *foie gras* in the pan to cook. Cook until it's tobacco yellow, but not grey or showing signs of blood – about a minute on each side. Serve the fritter with the *foie gras* on top.

sweetcorn relish for burgers

An old mate of mine, chef Andy Campbell, did a stint with me on *Saturday Kitchen*. He asked me if I wanted to see the easiest and best burger relish in the world. 'Of course', I replied. Here it is. Make your own mind up about the quantities of the last 3 ingredients; it's up to you what you spread on your burger!

serves 4

2 sweetcorn cobs
2 mangoes
3 tbsp finely chopped parsley
2 habañero chillies, deseeded and chopped
black pepper

Hold the cobs upright and slice off the yellow kernels. Bring a pan of salted water to the boil. Add the kernels and cook for 5 minutes. Drain well and set aside.

Peel and stone the mangoes and mash the flesh to a pulp. Add all the other ingredients, including the cooked sweetcorn, to the pulp. Cover and leave to sit, for the flavours to mingle, for 1 hour.

tomatoes

OK, I know tomatoes are a fruit, but we all use them like a vegetable, which is why I'm including them. I was lucky enough to work for a day with tomato pickers on the slopes of Vesuvius in Italy. That sounds so show-offish, doesn't it? The famed plum tomato San Marzano grows fantastically in the rich volcanic soil there. That day I had probably the simplest but most memorable lunch ever. We had wine, salami, cheese and bread. We picked basil and rocket that had been planted by pickers years before for the same reason. Then we picked the plum tomatoes. I don't think tomatoes have ever tasted so good!

I've lost count of the number of people who tell me that tomatoes taste so much better abroad, and that we can't grow a decent tomato in England. That is rubbish! The reason a tomato tastes better on holiday is almost certainly because it was picked that morning, and picked ripe at that. The tomatoes many of us buy from the supermarkets these days are likely to have been picked unripe a few days beforehand, and then we stick them in the fridge at home for another few days. I can assure you, if you get your hands on tomatoes just pulled ripe from a plant grown in England they will taste every bit as good as the ones you had on holiday.

It is no use buying fruit flown over from Venezuela in the middle of an English winter and thinking you're going to get anything near tasty. Imagine a young Neapolitan on his scooter in the middle of July looking forward to mama's Lancashire hotpot or a big, steaming vindaloo. Ridiculous isn't it? So why, in the middle of February, are we trying to create a basil, tomato and mozzarella salad? Instead, why not preserve tomatoes in the summer? In Spain and Italy you'll find jars and tins of them in most kitchens.

Please don't refrigerate tomatoes. I'm serious. They don't like it. It impairs their flavour, reducing them to tasteless water. When I bring home tomatoes I leave them in the sun if I can – let the sun get to them so that they seriously soften and the skins wrinkle and you will really get flavour! If you watch the veg being delivered to restaurants in the morning in Spain or Italy you'll be extremely unlikely to see a refrigerated vehicle.

One gripe I have is those little bits of red tomatoes you find floating in sauces in posh restaurants – this sauce is called *tomates concassées*. These tomatoes are skinned, the seeds and innards are taken out, and then what's left is diced up. Unfortunately, most of the tomato flavour is in that little jelly that surrounds the seed.

types of tomatoes

Trying to give a definitive guide to tomato varieties would be sheer folly. It is impossible to say what hybrid of tomato you might find in the shops. There are thousands of varieties out there. Even if I could describe each one, its flavour and texture would vary considerably depending on how long it had been allowed to

| jan | feb | mar | apr | may | jun | jul | aug | sep | oct | nov | dec |

ripen before being picked, how long it had spent in storage or transportation, the effect of gas flushing, the use of chemicals, what it had been fed with, the soil it had stood in, and what temperature you store it at after purchase. Nevertheless, here is the most accurate guide I can give to different groups of tomatoes.

Beef tomatoes: these have very thick flesh. They can be cut up for salads or for cooking, but are also big enough to be stuffed and eaten cold or stuffed and baked.

Cherry tomatoes: I have eaten some very sweet cherry tomatoes, but I have also eaten plum tomatoes that were sweeter than most of the cherry tomatoes I have tasted. If stretched, I would say that cherry tomatoes can be sweeter. They can be used either raw or cooked.

Plum tomatoes: these normally have a very firm flesh, less liquid and fewer seeds than round tomatoes. This makes them very good for cooking, and in particular for sauces.

Round or salad tomatoes: the vast number of varieties makes any advice I could give on flavour useless. Unfortunately there are now so many bad ones around that I avoid them completely.

Baby plum tomatoes: these are a bit of a novelty. I would use them in salads rather than cook with them, unless you have some that are at least as big as an egg,

Yellow cherry tomatoes: one of the finest tomatoes I ever tasted was a yellow 'sungold' picked straight from the plant in a sun-soaked garden in Dorset.

a few facts about tomatoes

Tomatoes are native to America. No one knows who brought them to Europe, but the first ones are believed to have been little cherry ones and yellow at that. The Spanish took them to Naples in the 16th century.

History recalls that the Neapolitan cook Francesco Leonardi first matched pasta with tomatoes in the 1700s, and then cooked meatballs in a tomato sauce soon afterwards. If only the Neapolitans had copyrighted this they would now have one of the richest regions of Europe.

buying tomatoes

Don't go for tomatoes on the vine. Actually, it's not a vine, it's a truss. All tomatoes come on a truss; you cannot grow tomatoes without them. It's true that when you open the bag you get a richer, deeper tomato fragrance, but this comes from the truss, not the fruit. A rubbish fruit is a rubbish fruit, whether it's on a vine or not. I once saw a packet of tomatoes on the vine that cost twice as much money as the other

tomatoes, and they had a 'grown for flavour' sticker proudly displayed across the packet. How thoughtful! What should they be grown for? Their ability to bounce?

storing tomatoes

Please don't refrigerate tomatoes; they don't like it. Let them sit in the sun. Also, don't buy them during the winter; rely, like I do, on tinned tomatoes or jars of passata instead.

peeling tomatoes

Drop the tomatoes into a bowl of boiling water. Leave for 2 minutes, then drain. The skins will peel off easily.

frying tomatoes

Halve the tomatoes. Melt some butter in a frying pan over a medium heat. When it is hot, add the tomatoes cut-side down. When they are brown on the cut side, turn them over for a couple more minutes.

Try with: a full English breakfast.

grilling tomatoes

Halve the tomatoes or cut them into thick slices, then brush them with olive oil. Heat a ridged char-grill pan to smoking hot, then add the tomatoes. When they are brown on one side, turn them over and cook the other side for a couple more minutes.

Try: on good toast.

roasting tomatoes

Preheat the oven to 220°C/425°F/gas mark 7. Use whole tomatoes, any kind, any size. Place the tomatoes in a roasting tin, drizzle them with olive oil and sprinkle on salt and pepper. Place them in the oven until they have browned. The tomatoes will normally split, but this is fine.

Try with: poached or grilled white fish.

tomato tarts

These are splendid little tarts, I can't quite understand how something so easy can impress so much! This is one of my favourite recipes to cook – it is just, well, so satisfying. Sticky cheese and light pastry are balanced by the tomato juice, and the pesto underneath leaves a garlicky tang on your tongue.

serves 4

375g (13oz) ready-rolled puff pastry

100g (3½oz) goat's cheese

tomatoes, sliced (the number of tomatoes depends on size; enough to cover the tarts)

4 tbsp pesto

a little olive oil

1 tbsp oregano, chopped

1 tbsp rosemary, chopped

salt and black pepper

Preheat the oven to 220°C/425°F/gas mark 7. Oil a baking tray.

Use a small plate or saucer to cut 4 circles out of the pastry. Put the circles on the baking tray.

Cut a deep circular groove 2cm (¾ inch) within the circumference of each round, but do not to cut all the way through the pastry.

Spread the pesto evenly within the inner circles formed by the grooves. Crumble the cheese over the pesto. Place the tomato slices on the cheese, being careful not to go past the groove; you want that edge to rise.

Dip a finger in some olive oil and wipe it around the empty edge of pastry until all the edge is coated. Sprinkle over the herbs and season with salt and pepper. Bake for 20–25 minutes.

basic tomato sauce

This is the only tomato sauce I like to have with pasta. It should be lovely and thick when you serve it.

serves 4

1kg (2lb 4oz) tomatoes

25g (1oz) butter

1 onion, finely chopped

2 cloves of garlic, crushed

2 rashers streaky bacon, chopped

1 large carrot, grated

4 tbsp sherry

1 bouquet garni

1 tsp caster sugar

2 tbsp tomato purée

Drop the tomatoes into a bowl of boiling water, leave for 2 minutes, then drain. Peel and chop them.

Melt the butter in a heavy-based pan over a medium heat. Add the onion, garlic and bacon and cook gently until the onion is soft. Add the remaining ingredients and season with salt and pepper.

Bring to the boil, then simmer, uncovered, for 45 minutes, stirring the sauce often.

tomato goulash

This is an easy and satisfying dish. You can have the whole thing in the oven in under 20 minutes. Be sure to use very fresh paprika.

serves 4-6

1kg (2lb 4oz) tomatoes

4 tbsp vegetable oil

900g (2lb) stewing steak, cut into 2.5cm (1 inch) cubes

salt and black pepper

1 onion, finely chopped

2 cloves of garlic, crushed

3 green peppers, deseeded and diced

2 tbsp paprika

1 tbsp finely chopped parsley

$^1/_2$ tbsp roughly chopped marjoram

2 tsp granulated sugar

Drop the tomatoes into a bowl of boiling water, leave for 2 minutes, then drain. Peel and chop them. Put to one side, covered.

Heat the oil in a frying pan over a medium heat. Add the stewing steak and fry until it is brown all over. Season well.

Transfer the meat to a pot with a lid, leaving the oil in the frying pan. Return the pan to the heat. When the oil is hot, add the onion and garlic and fry for 3 minutes. Add the peppers, sprinkle on the paprika and fry for 3 more minutes.

Transfer the onions, garlic and peppers to the pot containing the meat and place over a medium heat. Add the tomatoes and stir in the herbs. Bring to the boil. Add the sugar and season to taste. Cover and simmer for 1$^1/_2$ hours, until the meat is tender.

tomato and honey chicken

This is a treat and no mistake.

serves 4

1.5kg (3lb 5oz) tomatoes

2 tbsp vegetable oil

25g (1oz) butter

8 chicken thighs, seasoned

1 onion, grated

2 cloves of garlic, crushed

1 tsp powdered cinnamon

$^1/_2$ tsp grated fresh ginger

2 tbsp clear honey

salt and black pepper

Drop the tomatoes into a bowl of boiling water, leave for 2 minutes, then drain. Peel and chop them. Put to one side, covered.

Heat the oil and butter together in a heavy-based pot with a lid over a medium heat. Add the seasoned chicken thighs and cook until they have browned. And the onion, garlic, cinnamon, ginger and tomatoes. Season again.

Bring to the boil. Reduce the heat, cover and simmer for 1 hour, turning the chicken a couple of times while cooking.

Lift out the chicken thighs and set aside. Increase the heat and cook the sauce until it is thick – this will take about 20 minutes. Stir in the honey, then return the chicken to the pot and simmer until it has warmed through. Taste for seasoning.

toast-rack tomatoes

My children, Tom and Libby, enjoyed making this one. It looks really good in summer and the tastes are clean and fresh.

serves 4
4 eggs
4 big tomatoes
watercress, to serve

for the dressing
5 tbsp olive oil
1 tbsp red wine vinegar
salt and black pepper
a pinch of caster sugar
1 tbsp roughly chopped basil

Put the eggs in a small pan, cover with cold water and bring to the boil. Reduce to a simmer and cook, lid off, for 7 minutes. Cool the eggs under cold running water and peel when cold.

Using a serrated knife, cut the tomatoes into thick slices, cutting downwards to within 2.5cm (1 inch) of their base so they open up like a toast rack. Slice the boiled eggs to the same thickness and put a slice of egg in each tomato cut.

Mix all the dressing ingredients together.

Serve the tomatoes on a bed of watercress with some dressing poured over the top.

red tomato chutney

When I'm tasting up to 12 plates of food a day for *Masterchef Goes Large*, I simply cannot face another plate of food when I get home. Instead, I stock the larder with good cheeses and open a jar of this chutney.

makes 1kg
1.5kg (3lb 5oz) ripe tomatoes
450g (1lb) onions, finely chopped
1 tsp salt
1 tsp paprika
¼ tsp cayenne pepper
2 red chillies, finely chopped
150ml (5fl oz) spiced distilled or malt vinegar
175g (6oz) white or brown sugar

Drop the tomatoes into a bowl of boiling water, leave for 2 minutes, then drain. Peel and chop them.

Put the tomatoes and onions in a large, heavy-based pan over a medium heat. Bring to the boil, reduce the heat, and simmer, lid off, for 20-30 minutes, until soft. Add the salt, spices, chillies and half the vinegar and cook for another 45 minutes, until thick.

Add the sugar and the rest of the vinegar and cook, stirring all the time, until the sugar dissolves. Continue simmering until thick. Pot the chutney in sterilized, warm jars, and seal. Leave it to mature for at least a month before using.

stuffed tomatoes

Good olives are essential – none of those pre-pitted ones you can buy. The combination of the olives, sweet tomatoes, salty anchovies, and that unmistakable tang of basil is classic and irresistible....

serves 4

4 large beef tomatoes

16 small yellow cherry tomatoes

24 basil leaves

16 black olives, stoned and chopped

16 anchovy fillets in oil

8 tbsp olive oil

salt and black pepper

Preheat the oven to 200°C/400°F/gas mark 6.

Cut the beef tomatoes in half horizontally. Using a spoon, scoop out the flesh and discard, then put the shells in an ovenproof dish, all in one layer. Cut the cherry tomatoes in half.

Fill the cavities of the beef tomatoes with the cherries. For each beef tomato half, place 3 basil leaves on top of the cherry tomatoes, then sprinkle on some chopped olives, then add 2 anchovy fillets. Drizzle each tomato half with 1 tbsp olive oil. Season with pepper.

Bake in the oven for 15–20 minutes. Allow to cool before serving.

preserved tomatoes

You have no chance of getting a decent tomato in northern Europe in the winter. I don't care how many vines it's hanging off or which country you bought it from! You have to, like the clever people of the Mediterranean, learn to preserve your summer harvest.

plum tomatoes, quartered

olive oil

garlic, sliced

oregano

Preheat the oven 120°C/225°F/gas mark ¼.

Put the tomatoes on a baking tray and drizzle with a little oil.

Cook in the oven for 2½ hours, until the moisture has gone and the tomatoes are crispy. Allow to cool.

Place in a sterilized airtight jar. Add, per 1kg (2lb 4oz) of tomatoes, 1 garlic clove and ½ tbsp oregano, cover with oil and seal. You can keep them indefinitely.

tomato bruschetta

This is a good snack and an even better breakfast. That tang of garlic and the juiciness of good tomatoes spread over toast are delicious.

serves 4

4 large plum tomatoes
salt and black pepper
1 ciabatta loaf
olive oil, for brushing
1 large clove of garlic, halved

Finely dice the tomatoes, season them and leave to one side, covered, for 10 minutes.

Heat a grill-pan until it is really hot. Cut the ciabatta in half and slice through each half again. Brush one side with oil and place, oiled side down, in a pan. While it is cooking, brush the other side with oil. When one side is brown, turn over.

When both sides are brown, remove from the pan. Rub the garlic clove over the toasted bread. Cover with the chopped tomatoes and season with pepper.

tomato bulghur wheat salad

This should be a fridge standby for when you come in too tired or too drunk to cook. Definitely a summer dish and very good picnic food.

serves 4

125g (4½oz) bulghur wheat
600ml (1 pint) vegetable stock, boiling
250g (9oz) baby tomatoes
6 plum tomatoes
3 spring onions
2 tbsp chopped chives
2 tbsp roughly chopped mint
2 tbsp finely chopped parsley
salt and black pepper

Cover the wheat with the boiling stock and leave it to soak for 30 minutes, until the water is all absorbed. Drain if necessary. Leave to cool.

Roughly chop the tomatoes and finely chop the spring onions. Add them to the soaked wheat with the herbs, and season to taste.

turnips

Turnips are an acquired taste, and it is difficult to get children to eat them. But for me they are unbeatable. In stews or casseroles, cooked with care, they retain just enough of their crunch. But I also love them sliced up raw in a salad. I wasn't aware of the use of raw turnips until, when recording a programme for Radio 4's *Veg Talk*, a grower I was chatting to lifted up a turnip, wiped it with a cloth, then cut off a slice and stuck it in his mouth. 'Want a slice?' he asked, 'this will wake you up.'
It certainly did!

I had no idea how peppery that innocent-looking veg could be. When I'm at the farm during the turnip season, I always chew a few slices of raw turnip – the crunch, juice and heat are a real pick-me-up. Turnips are a brassica, which means they are related to the cabbage. In fact, if you leave any brassica (and this includes the turnip) alone and let them reproduce naturally, they will eventually revert back to type and become a wild cabbage.

The tops of turnips are edible, bordering on delicious. I see them as a nicely course green, not dissimilar to a spring green, and I'm happy to serve them up with a roast.

types of turnip

Don't always look for bright, white flesh; yellowing of a turnip's flesh is not a sign of age. Turnips go from bright white to yellow and their stalks may be green or purple. They are at their sweetest when very young – they still have that sharpness, but they are very sweet. So go for small, young turnips if you want that sweetness; as a rule, if you buy anything bigger than a ping pong ball and you are losing sweetness and the texture and taste becomes coarser. There is no need to peel turnips that are smaller than a ping-pong ball.

a few facts about turnips

Known as a wild plant in Europe in prehistoric times, the turnip was cultivated very early. It is thought to have originated in northern Europe in about 2,000BC from a variety of rape. Today turnip cultivation has spread to most parts of the world.

buying turnips

Always feel turnips before you buy; they should be solid and have no give or sponginess. Look out for wrinkling on the skin too, as this is a sure sign of age.

storing turnips

Winter turnips will keep up to 2 months in a cool place.

buttering turnips

Peel the turnips, then dice them into 2cm (¾ inch) chunks, dropping them into acidulated water as you go (if they are small, only trim the root and stalk and wash).

jan	feb	mar	apr	may	jun	jul	aug	sep	oct	nov	dec

Bring a pan of salted water to the boil. Drain the turnips, drop them into the boiling water and boil, lid off, for 5 minutes. Drain. Melt a large knob of butter in a frying pan and, when hot, add the turnips. Cook, uncovered, over a medium heat for 5–8 minutes, until golden, turning while cooking. Rosemary will add flavour if added at start of frying.

Try with: chicken or turkey

cooking turnips in cream

Prepare and cook as for buttering. Once your turnips are nicely coloured and cooked, add a little single cream and a few chopped chives.

Try with: duck

mashing turnips

Peel the turnips, then chop them into 2cm (¾ inch) cubes. Bring a pan of salted water to the boil. Add the turnips and boil, lid off, for 20 minutes, until soft. Do not boil too hard as root veg will break up with rough handling. Drain well, return to the pan and mash it up, keeping it as rough as you can handle. Add butter and salt, to taste, and lots of pepper, then stir – the amount of butter you use depends on what texture you want.

Try with: haggis

roasting turnips

Preheat the oven to 190°C/375°F/gas mark 5. Peel the turnips and cut them into sticks 2cm thick, dropping them into acidulated water as you go. Bring a pan of salted water to the boil. Drain the turnips, drop them in the boiling water and boil, lid off, for 5 minutes. Drain. Pour a little vegetable oil in a roasting tin and preheat it in the oven. When the oil is hot, add the turnips and roast for 40 minutes, turning occasionally.

Try with: a joint of meat

glazing baby turnips

Peel and trim the baby turnips and wash. Bring a pan of salted water to the boil. Drop in the turnips and boil for 8 minutes, until just cooked. Drain all but 2 tbsp of water, keeping the turnips in the pan with the reserved water. Add 2 tsp caster sugar and cook over a low heat, stirring, until the sugar has dissolved. Stir in some butter and cook over a high heat until the turnips are coated and glazed. Shake the pan to prevent sticking.

Try with: roast duck

turnip and rocket salad

It was on an outside broadcast for Radio 4 that I first tasted a raw turnip. It was a grower who insisted I do so, and I'm glad he did. Try it, it's peppery and crunchily refreshing at the same time. I love the citrus taste of sorrel leaves, but experiment with your own leaf variations. I deliberately left this dish bereft of colour.

serves 4

500g (1lb 2oz) turnips, washed

100g (3¹/₂oz) sorrel leaves

100g (3¹/₂oz) rocket leaves

for the dressing

100ml (3¹/₂fl oz) olive oil

juice of 1 lemon

1 tbsp Dijon mustard

salt and black pepper

Slice the turnips very thinly.

For the dressing, mix all the ingredients to taste; this is your dressing!

In a bowl, mix the sliced turnips with the sorrel leaves and rocket. Pour over the dressing.

spiced turnips with spinach and tomatoes

This salad offers a good combination of textures, flavours and colours.

serves 6

450g (1lb) well-flavoured tomatoes

4 tbsp olive oil

2 onions, thinly sliced

450g (1lb) baby turnips, halved

1 tsp caster sugar

1 tsp paprika

4 tbsp chopped parsley

10g basil, torn into bits

450g (1lb) spinach, stalks removed

salt and black pepper

Drop the tomatoes into a bowl of boiling water, leave for 2 minutes, then drain. Peel and chop them.

Heat the olive oil in large frying pan. Add the onions and fry over a medium heat until golden.

Add the turnips, chopped tomatoes, sugar and paprika to the pan and cook until the tomatoes are broken down – about 10 minutes. Cover the pan and continue to cook for another 10 minutes, or until the turnips are tender.

Stir in the parsley, basil and spinach. Season and cook for another 3 minutes. Serve warm or cold.

ragoût of lamb with turnips

This dish tastes best if refrigerated, then reheated and eaten the day after it is cooked. Browning the lamb, onions and turnips well will really boost the flavour of this dish.

serves 6

2 tbsp vegetable oil

1kg (2lb 4oz) shoulder of lamb, cut into 2.5cm (1 inch) cubes

4 onions, quartered

1 tbsp plain flour

1 bouquet garni

1 clove of garlic, crushed

2 stalks celery, finely sliced

250ml (9fl oz) lamb, chicken or vegetable stock

25g (1oz) butter

500g (1lb 2oz) small white turnips, quartered

salt and black pepper

6 medium potatoes

Preheat the oven to 180°C/350°F/gas mark 4.

Heat the oil in a frying pan over a medium heat. When it is hot, add the lamb to brown all over. Do not overcrowd the pan. Once it is brown, add the onions and continue to fry until they are brown. Add the flour and cook, stirring, for 2 minutes.

Transfer the lamb and onions to a casserole dish and add the bouquet garni, garlic and celery. Pour in the stock. Bring to the boil, stirring, cover, and leave to simmer.

Meanwhile, add the butter to the used frying pan over a medium heat and, when medium hot, add the turnips. Cook until browned, then season and add to the casserole.

Cook in the oven for 1½ hours. Peel and halve the potatoes. Add them to the casserole, season, and return to the oven for a further 45 minutes, or until both the lamb and potatoes are tender. Remove the bouquet garni before serving.

glazed turnips and a duck

I know I should be banging on about the turnips here, glazed yellow and sticky. They are a delight, and this is one of my favourite ways of eating them. The duck, though, as a good duck should, steals the show. I get a feeling of smugness bordering on delight when I cook such a grown-up dish.

serves 4

1.5kg (3lb 5oz) duck

100g (3½oz) butter

1 onion, finely chopped

1 carrot, chopped

1 stalk celery, sliced

250ml (9fl oz) dry white wine

1 bouquet garni

salt and black pepper

12 small white turnips, quartered

12 small white onions

2 tbsp granulated sugar

250ml (9fl oz) chicken stock

2 tsp cornflour

Preheat the oven to 190°C/375°F/gas mark 5.

Remove any excess fat from inside the duck.

In a flameproof casserole dish, melt 25g (1oz) butter over a medium heat. Add the duck and cook, turning it in the hot butter, until brown all over. Remove the duck and put it to one side.

Tip the fat out of the casserole, leaving just 1 tbsp. Put the pan back on the heat. Add the onion, carrot and celery and cook, lid on, until soft – about 10 minutes.

Place the duck on top of the frying vegetables. Add the white wine and bouquet garni and season well. Cover the casserole with a lid and place in the oven for 1½ hours.

About 20 minutes before the end of the cooking time, put the turnips and white onions in a heavy-bottomed saucepan. Add the sugar, remaining butter and stock. Cook, lid on, until the turnips are nearly soft, about 15 minutes. Remove the lid and continue cooking until nearly all the liquid has reduced. You can roll the pan, but don't stir it or you will break up the turnips. You want a sticky yellow coating on your veg.

Take the duck from the casserole and check it is cooked. Plonk it on your serving dish. Strain the liquid from the casserole into a clean pan. Add 2 tbsp water to the cornflour and stir until smooth. Place the pan of strained juices on a medium heat and add the cornflour mix. Bring the pan to the boil, simmer for 5 minutes, and season to taste.

Surround the duck with the glazed turnips and onions. Serve with the gravy.

index

acknowledgements

Thanks to Vernon, without whose help I would never have had the time to write this book; to Rosemary, who looks after everything I do; to Dixie, without whom I would never have done anything; to Denise, who lends her support still; and to Amanda, for doing what only Amanda can do.